Planning for the intelligent accessing of income in retirement is the most important, yet sadly, the most underutilized discipline in the industry today"

BROOK HANSEN, PRESIDENT:
CREATIVE WEALTH STRATEGIES

"Brook Hansen is a no-nonsense, highly knowledgeable, articulate and proven wealth creation strategist. Within the confines of his book, Brook unlocks and explains, in simplistic fashion and with specific pragmatic examples, the intrinsic elements of the Uniform Prudent Investor Act (UPIA) as a guideline for wealth creation and management for those who are willing to listen and learn. For years, the UPIA has been used by the wealthy and the ultra-wealthy to maximize wealth creation by strategically managing one's assets for both maximum growth and minimum tax burden. Brook's book clearly allows for a lay audience to take advantage of the same tactics used by the wealthy under the UPIA to achieve long-term wealth while legally minimizing the tax burdens that accompany sustained wealth creation."

CHARLES N. BLITZER
PRESIDENT AND CEO, BARBEAU PHARMA, INC.

"Brook distills many years of experience into this concise road map for wealth creation"

BILL HUEFNER ESQ
BARNA, GUZY & STEFFEN

Developing Financial Intelligence

Taking the assets you already have, and making them financially efficient

WRITTEN BY
R. Brook Hansen CLU, ChFC, AEP

Bloomington, IN   authorHOUSE™   Milton Keynes, UK

AuthorHouse™
1663 Liberty Drive, Suite 200
Bloomington, IN 47403
www.authorhouse.com
Phone: 1-800-839-8640

AuthorHouse™ UK Ltd.
500 Avebury Boulevard
Central Milton Keynes, MK9 2BE
www.authorhouse.co.uk
Phone: 08001974150

First published by AuthorHouse 3/17/2006

ISBN: 1-4259-2350-X (sc)

Printed in the United States of America
Bloomington, Indiana

This book is printed on acid-free paper.

Securities and advisory services offered through Workman Securities, Inc., member NASD, SIPC, and a Registered Investment Advisor. Creative Wealth Strategies and Workman Securities, Inc are separate and unrelated companies.

I am dedicating this book to my clients, because you have either taught me or caused me to learn virtually everything I know about wealth creation and maintenance. I sincerely appreciate your loyalty, patience and support.

TABLE OF CONTENTS

SEEKING A FINANCIAL PLANNING STRUCTURE

I have spent the last couple of my 10+ years as a financial advisor seeking a way to "mass customize" the concept of creating a financial planning constitution that individuals can use to establish the proper framework for a successful financial future.

The reason I refer to this concept as a "constitution" is that it makes sense that we all operate based on certain truths that are, or should be, subject to amendment.

A friend of mine has an analogy for this concept: Guardrails on a high bridge. If the longest, highest bridge you ever drove across had no guardrails, how fast would you drive on that bridge? Would you drive on it at all? Have you ever actually hit a guardrail while driving over a bridge? Probably not, but the fact remains that the lack of a guardrail affects your speed, and your willingness to, cross the bridge.

The same concept holds true in our financial lives. We have boundaries that we either developed or inherited as they relate to what we're willing to do in order to create or use our wealth wisely. Few people consider how to use those boundaries to accelerate their processes and progress toward their goals.

So my thought process went like this: If I could create a flexible enough planning outline, I could better serve my clients and teach the concepts to other advisers so that they can better serve their clients, and so on. A consistent, yet flexible financial constitution is also a tool to distribute these ideas to individuals outside my sphere of influence through a medium other than individual consulting.

I have been writing narratives through the years for the benefit of my clients and myself, and a great deal of the content of this book is a collection of that previously-created intellectual capital. I will talk in this book about developing infrastructure and intellectual assets, and these works are excellent examples of creating a solution to one issue while creating foundations for other tools. It is part and parcel of the concept that we need to invest our time and treasure in assets that create multiple benefits. Another benefit of writing narratives is that is causes us to think deeply about the ideas we are trying to get across. It helps the author crystallize thinking; and in my case, to provide better advice in my daily practice by having thought carefully through the aspects of the subject matter in order to convey the ideas thoughtfully, thoroughly and clearly, in print.

It is true of your planning, as well. Writing down near- and long-term goals and the steps you have taken or need to take to achieve them is the beginning of the process. Just doing that puts you ahead of the curve. Read a book on effective goal setting; Bryan Tracy has several that will set you on the right path. But, begin with the exercise of identifying the opportunities at hand. I will flush out a few of these in the chapter on Ancillary Business Activities.

As often happens, the answer to my long-time focus was delivered in the form of a solution for multiple issues within my businesses. We recently took on the responsibility of Third Party Asset Management for the registered representatives of our broker/dealer and some larger profit sharing-type plans, and were seeking to communicate the methodology we use to manage assets (i.e., Modern Portfolio Theory). We also had an ethical dilemma as it related to the scope of our delegation. It has always been easy to operate as a fiduciary for our clients. We know them and their circumstances. We manage their entire trust estate and understand the ramifications of the decisions we are making. How were we to maintain that standard for people inside a largish pension plan? Our business model simply could not withstand that kind of influx of clients, nor does it make sense for it to do so. **A citadel asset of our firm is that we will do no harm.** When I was trying to figure out how I could serve those that I do not know, considering that when I am investing their assets I am doing so without the knowledge of whether or not they should even be investing in this plan, made me uncomfortable. What I discovered is that this tool --this book along with DVDs and other materials that make up a larger financial intelligence package -- allows us to educate those for whom our responsibility is limited to equities management within their retirement plan, and also allows us to expand our education to people completely outside of our sphere of influence.

The asset management technique I referred to earlier, Modern Portfolio Theory (MPT), will be discussed in more detail in Chapter 2. To elicit support for this theory, we read the Uniform Prudent Investor Act (UPIA). We knew that Modern Portfolio Theory had a great deal to do with the creation of the UPIA, but had not read past the Prefatory Note, which was all I needed to read previously to convince me I was on the right track.

After going through the Act word for word several times I discovered within it the constitution I was looking for. Not only did it validate my choice of asset management techniques, it embraced the "entire trust" concept we use in our practice and it provides, either directly or subtly, the framework for the creation of an excellent financial plan.

The concepts surrounding the Act, blended with the financial tools presented here and the opportunities your individual circumstances afford, form the framework and tools to build an excellent financial plan.

It is important to note that these are ideas I cannot take credit for. The UPIA is not a third party endorsement of MY way of doing business. It's quite the opposite. I have been unconsciously competent as it relates to implementing the majority of the standards prescribed by the Act. It is time for me, and you, to consciously apply the Act's principles. The authors of this Act obviously gave a great deal of thought as to how it impacts trusts and their beneficiaries. It is up to me to help you understand that you and your collection of assets are the trust, and that you and your family are its beneficiaries. The Act has within it the bones of every financial plan ever entered into, either accidentally or on purpose, successful or disastrous. To think that this was created by attorneys and accepted by politicians blows my mind.

So who am I and why should my interpretation matter? My name is Robert Brook Hansen, but I go by Brook. My wife since 1983 is Debbie. We have three kids, a boy and twin daughters. I like to think we are happy. I have been an entrepreneur of one kind or another since I was 16 and purchased my first fast food franchise at age 25. I was adopted at birth by an excellent family and at age 22 met my "Bio-Mother." I graduated in 1981 and my folks gave me what I have come to call my $100 scholarship. They gave me $100 and two cases of Old Style Beer and suggested that the oil patch might be a good place to seek work. I headed west (I lived in Wisconsin at the time) and found myself living under a bridge. I had a friend with a 1968 Dodge who came along and "rescued" me, so I was able to live for a while in the Dodge under the bridge. That was an "upgrade" from the time I spent hitchhiking around with a six pack of beer (very effective). I made a living and returned to collect my bride and "escape" for good. We sold the franchise at age 29 (10 years after leaving the bridge) and discovered for the first time the effects of not managing your taxes or the method you used to sell assets. It was an expensive lesson but one that bore fruit later on. I then went to work with a substantial regional restaurant chain as a manager and within 18 months had created the job of Director of Delivery Operations, which involved the task of implementing delivery in the company's 25 restaurants. That was a "job" and, as such, could only take me so far. The next step was to go to work for the Tax Reduction Institute, where I sold and instructed courses on offensive tax reduction. It was a limited role, but as I describe in a later chapter, it led me to the financial services industry in 1995. I was extremely fortunate in that the firm I chose to work with had a culture that demanded education in the industry and I took that to heart. In 20 months

4

I earned both my Chartered Financial Consultant (ChFC) and my Chartered Life Underwriter (CLU) designations, adding the Accredited Estate Planner (AEP) designation a couple of years later. I have had the opportunity to implement dozens of advanced financial plans and am considered an expert in this area. I am a third party asset manager utilized by Trusts, Broker/Dealers and Pension Plans, and have been managing assets using Modern Portfolio Theory since 1996. I have had the pleasure of teaching for the Society of Financial Services Professionals, the National Association of Financial and Insurance Planners, the Minneapolis and other Boards of Realtors, as well as many other "regional" organizations. My focus is primarily client education and plan implementation.

Why does any of that matter to you? I have gleaned experience from hundreds of people and their circumstances and have studied vast amounts of data to support financial solutions. I have developed context over the years by borrowing on the experience of others and never repeating the same year of experience. Ever. Consequently, I offer the wisdom and experience of many successful people.

The entire Act is printed at the end of this writing, but we are going to go through the Act in the next chapter in some detail, working pretty much from beginning to end, explaining how it applies to you along the way. The language that is pulled specifically from the Act will be in italics. My interpretation or "framing" of the intent will not. Following the chapter on the Act we will go through a number of potential tools to achieve the goals the Act sets forth.

I am not setting out to create a best seller here. What follows will NOT be a soft, entertaining story with some useful thoughts thrown in. That will be left to others. This is an effort to deliver as much quality, actionable information to the reader in the most concise manner I can muster. As such, it is written pretty tightly. You should expect to have to read sentences or paragraphs more than once to understand the meaning and place it into context. You should read this with a pencil and a highlighter, writing down questions as you go. I may answer the question directly, indirectly or not at all, somewhere later in the book, but thoughtful questioning of the content and context will help you get the most from this writing. You should note the names of people that something reminds you of, or assets that you have that an idea may apply to. If you are in the accumulation phase, certain alarms may go off. Write them down. Your notes in the margins may be the best training you get from this. We need to mine your skills, relationships, passions and assets in an effort to get the best results. Only one of those things is tangible, so it is what comes from WITHIN you that may be most compelling.

Be prepared to read this book more than once. One of my clients, Projects Done Write, has been good enough to work with me on editing this book. In our meetings she said, "I learned a lot. I would read something and say, 'Oh, *that's* what he was talking about.'" The information struck her as if it was the first time she had heard it. It was, but not because she had not been presented the words before. She has had the benefit of implementing some of the strategies and *then* reading the material. It was new material to her in some ways, or expanded the ideas that were tugging at the edges of her mind. You will receive the same benefit and a larger impact if, after reading this book and implementing the ideas, you set a date to re-read it one year out. You will be amazed at how far you have come and how much it expands and cements positive trends. I have had the joy of watching it happen in my business for a decade now.

Roll up your sleeves. I hope you enjoy it.

The Prefatory Note of the Act refers to several changes that have taken place over the past decades that caused the Act's creation. One of the concepts that drove the investment portion of the Act is the idea that a prudent man would invest his money in such a way as to achieve the highest expected return based on the risk he is willing to take. Where this seems obvious it is important to understand that until Harry Markowitz discovered and perfected the concepts supporting Modern Portfolio Theory, there was essentially no measurable way to accomplish this while investing in equities. Hence the prudent man rule often limited investments for fiduciaries to cash, preferred stocks, bonds and the like. It was after 40 more years of study and earning the Nobel Prize did this become considered an attainable goal.

Where at first glance it may seem as though the Act is focused on equities investments, there is a theme sounded over and over again that the prudent investor must take all assets, liabilities and conditions of the beneficiaries into consideration in order to determine whether or not a decision is suitable. It also appears at first that the Act refers specifically and exclusively to Trusts.

What is a Trust? There are dozens of types of trusts, but for our purposes and for the most part, a trust is a collection of assets intended to provide benefits for current income beneficiaries with the remaining trust assets intended to provide for remainder beneficiaries (AKA the heirs). Read that again.

Aren't a retired couple, a family and a business also trusts? Yes, although they're not usually structured or thought of that way. If you are a retired person you have income producing assets of various types, all taxable in one form or another, as well as non-income producing assets that either provide lifestyle benefits or are being deferred for future use. You are the current income beneficiaries and your heirs are the remainder beneficiaries.

This is a long way of saying that this Act pertains to you. No court will punish you for not following the Act's recommendations, but you may be punished financially. You are the trustee of your trust; as such, it is your responsibility to make sure its income beneficiaries are happy and well served. Consider that this is an art form and that you and all of your resources, your actual assets and the various financial tools and options, are your palette of many colors. The better your understanding of what you want the picture to look like, and the better your understanding of the brushes and pigments you have to work with, the better your outcome will be.

THE ACT'S OBJECTIVES:

I cannot emphasize enough the importance of the Act's **first objective:** *The trustee must take the entirety of the trust into account.* All assets, whether intellectual, physical, spiritual or real estate, come into play when creating the proper plan. You are the material with which you have to work.

a) There are things you love to do and things you hate to do.

b) You have an excellent work ethic as it relates to your finances; or, you do not.

c) You like getting involved in projects to create wealth, understanding that you can leverage more that way; or, you prefer to work hard in your job or business and save your way to security.

d) You understand that the key to the creation of significant wealth is the acquisition and management of debt, and you embrace the path of leverage; or, the concept of multiple debts scares you into inactivity.

e) You have a long history of living within your means; or, you cannot even spell budget.

All of these things are the assets of the trust and are more important than the value of the second home, the mutual funds or the IRA. Developing an understanding of what your "guardrails" are will allow you to create a list of your passions, skills, goals and limitations, enabling you to create a plan you will actually execute and continue.

Your skills, relationships, current assets and fears are your beginning point. Write them down; they may surprise you. If you're married, do it separately and then look to fill gaps.

The **second objective** of the Act is to underline that: *The trade off between risk and return is to be the fiduciary's central consideration.*

This is a bold statement, particularly when taking objective one into consideration. The tradeoff between risk and return is your primary consideration. In your equities portfolio the Act does a pretty good job of conveying that the use of Modern Portfolio Theory (MPT) will have that effect, but how does this impact the rest of the trust? Just what are the risks you are trying to balance against?

PORTFOLIO RISK:

We will cover this as it relates to equities in more detail later on, but everyone invested in anything has portfolio risk. Markets move. That's why they work, and your portfolio is no exception. Your own businesses, insurance policies, ability to earn, variable or fixed debt, geographic location of and equity in real estate, make up the balance of the estate. Lifestyle expenses (i.e. staying alive and paying the bills) are the constant drain on that portfolio.

CURRENT TAXATION:

If you are alive this concerns you. It does not matter if you are a young family, retired couple, small business or an old curmudgeon. Taxes matter.

ere are darn few things you can impact in this financial world we navigate, and managing the extent and timing of our taxation is one of the most important things we can do. Investing in assets that create tax deferral may substantially reduce taxation for a middle income retired couple based on the current rules on taxation of social security. If you are a high-income employee with a propensity to save in mutual funds, bank accounts and/or 401(k) type investments, you are paying most of the taxes in this country. Thank you.

If you would like to discontinue this practice, consider purchasing a few single-family homes as rentals. It seems reasonable you would purchase more "high end" properties. They may barely cash flow, even with a decent down payment, but they grow tax-deferred and throw off another important thing -- depreciation deductions.

You can deduct depreciation on a single-family home over 27 years. In the Minneapolis market, a high-end single family home that would be suitable as a rental may cost as much as $325,000. Since I like simplicity let's say that $270,000 is considered building and, as such, is depreciable. Dividing the $270,000 by 27 years creates a $10,000-per-year tax deduction for each property. If you owned three properties you would create $30,000 in deductions year after year. If you purchased one per year for three years, in the fourth year you still get the deduction. You may or may not be able to take these deductions every year, depending upon your other income and circumstances, but it will offset rents and income produced by your mutual funds year after year, and someday you will have appreciated, low-debt, tax-favored assets to sell (or not) for income. By the way, what is your deduction the year after you stop contributing to your 401(k), and how tax-favored is the income you eventually derive from it?

The family that has a few different sources of income should consider accessing income at intervals. Every three years take a distribution of IRA assets, pay a little more in taxes on the IRA that year, put the balance in the bank and live on that along with social security income for three years. You may not have to pay tax at all on your social security income for two of the three years. The effective tax savings is enormous and it impacts your overall return on investments. Not paying $10,000 in taxes over two years will create a rate of return larger on the withdrawn amount than the market will likely give (given the facts as stated, the withdrawal would be less than $75,000). At $75,000 the taxes saved on social security income would represent over 13%, and the bank will pay something. These numbers are not scientific and everyone is different. The point is that your rate of return is on that of the *entire* trust, and every action has a reaction.

We are going to get into more depth regarding creating effective income plans a little further along, but this should get you interested in how income planning can affect you.

LIVING TOO LONG:
(SPENDING TOO MUCH OR INVESTING TOO CAUTIOUSLY)

This is the risk people take the most seriously, as well they should. Getting to the place where you are still alive and are out of assets is the scariest financial outcome on the radar. (I am not talking about a 50- or 60-year-old going bankrupt. This is 88 and out of money.) One of two things will get us there: Spending too much or investing too cautiously. Remember that the ability to learn, to earn and to navigate in financial transactions are all assets. Even if a person never earned much and lived a life where they seemed to spend little, they are in trouble if they did not take enough risk with the assets they had (even if abilities were all they had) and they still spent too much in relation to what they earned to allow them to save for retirement.

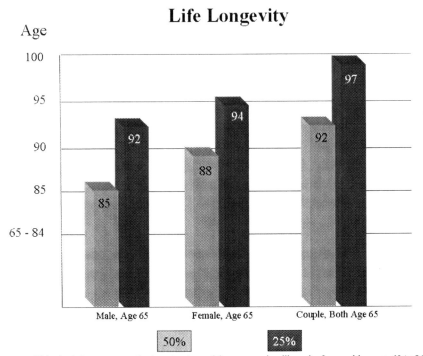

Life Longevity

This chart gives an approximate percentage of the age people will reach after reaching ages 65 to 84.

figure 1

Figure 1 shows the chances of living a very long time. It's pretty dramatic and when you consider the advancement of medical knowledge doubles every five years, it is likely this trend will continue or accelerate. We have to prepare to need money for a long time to avoid running out.

One of the practical things we can do to avoid either of these scenarios is to divide our assets into separate pools based on when we intend to access them. We would take less risk and more aggressively manage taxes on the money we were to use first. We would take moderate risk with the next pool to be accessed, managing taxes in practical ways. We would take more risk with the next-to-last assets to be accessed, potentially with some "hedges" in place, and still more risk with the last assets out of the corral. This will allow you to focus on the near-term from a tax perspective while investing in the middle-to-long-term in ways to allow tax flexibility and allow you to take more overall risk in your entire trust because you have a plan that has some certainty as well as flexibility built in. Again, we will give more details on this in income planning.

Dying too soon:

In this context, dying before you have your affairs in order is too soon. It is always too soon, isn't it? For just about everyone that means having a well-drafted Will or Trust as well as proper property ownership and beneficiary designations. If you are a family and your trust is not completely funded (i.e. you don't have enough wealth for the family to function) you probably need to add insurance to the formula. If you are a business owner you need buy-sell agreements and a well-communicated plan to run the business so it has some value when you are gone.

The balance of this discussion is outside of where I am going in this narrative, but remember that the tradeoff between risk and return is the fiduciary's central consideration; and dying too soon is a fundamental, undeniable risk.

I will cover the essentials of creating a well-drafted Will along with a couple of simple property ownership ideas that reduce estate taxes on assets you already own, after we cover the Act. You should review the Will section whether you have one in place or not, as it may give you additional food for thought.

Eventual Taxation:

Death and Taxes. The Act talks about income taxation in a trust in the event of the death of the trust's grantor (you) but does not talk about estate taxes because the trust represents an unnatural person who cannot die. BUT, because it talks about using care, skill and caution in dealing with assets affected by death, I will take the liberty of expanding that into estate taxes. Creating effective Wills and Trusts will go a long way toward minimizing taxes on a person's base wealth, and the way you own your property will ultimately have the largest impact on taxes at death. We will discuss a few of these ideas in more detail later. Our website has a number of articles on tax reduction and avoidance if you want additional ideas.

If your total net worth including death benefits is in the $2,000,000 or greater range, it would be a good idea to do some homework in this area. Another important aspect of eventual taxation relates to income taxes. IRAs, 401(k)s and the like will be taxed as withdrawn, as will the gains in annuity contracts, either favorably or unfavorably, whether you're alive or not. How you (and your heirs) access your income will have a larger effect on your total return than will securities selection and market timing combined. So, as you create your assets, invest energy in considering how you will access the income they will eventually be called upon to create.

Objective three indicates that: **_All potential investments may be suitable in achieving the risk-versus-return tradeoff if they meet the other requirements of prudent investing, based on the trust's larger circumstances._**

Once again, this includes investing in education; assets that only make sense from a satisfaction perspective; hedges against particular risks (living too long, for instance); and on and on. There was a time when trustees were not allowed to make certain types of investments no matter how they fit into the scheme of things. This objective embraces the idea that we need to explore all possible investment options in view of your skills and bias in favor or against certain things (debt acquisition, for instance).

Objective four: Duty to diversify investments.

The word duty is the one I find compelling and challenging as it relates to diversification. In my years of studying Markowitz's MPT and the supporting research, and implementing the strategy to the best of my ability, it is wonderful to see someone other than Markowitz referring to it that strongly. Markowitz goes so far as to "prove" in a 1957 paper "that no un-diversified portfolio would be favorable to a properly diversified portfolio." I understand that from an equities perspective but it can be hard to apply in "outside" investments. If you are in the accumulation phase it may make sense to be heavily weighted in leveraged real estate. You can and should create some diversification in the real estate you invest in, but I would hardly say you should invest an equal amount in equities or cash, etc. If you're a business owner in the accumulation phase I am going to council you to diversify within your business, invest in assets that support your business, hedge your bets and create some outside investments. But it rarely makes sense to stop having your company and/or your business be your primary investment. The investment that performs the best is invariably the one that creates the most leverage. Nothing has as many leverage points as owning your own business.

The duty to diversify as it relates to a typical trust is easier to justify than it is in an accumulation scenario, BUT diversification amongst growth assets, in which you may have invested a heavy concentration of your net worth, is highly advisable whether it be real estate, employer stock, or within your business.

Objective five indicates that: **_Delegation of certain duties is accepted_**. Later in the Act the narratives describe a trend that favors the delegation of some trust functions to professionals. In the past there has been at least some debate about fiduciaries allowing others to perform certain tasks. There are standards for delegation that we will cover toward the end of this chapter, but there are basic reasons to consider it:

- Professionals are held to a higher standard.

- There are certain tasks you may not want to perform.

- Some tasks may be impractical to perform.

- You may not have the skill sets to perform some tasks.

- If you are a fiduciary there may be "risks" you would prefer to shift.

15

Much of pages five and six of the Act refer you to reading and legislation that supports the Act's creation, much of it again directing us back to MPT, but it also spells out who is implicitly covered by the Act and who may be covered under the right circumstances. You can take a look at it but we have hopefully already ascertained that you are in charge of your own trust and this Act relates to you or it does not. It is likely that if you have read this far you understand its implications for you in your life.

Section One: Prudent Investor Rule

A trustee who invests and manages trust assets owes a duty to the beneficiaries of the trust to comply with the prudent investor rule set forth in this Act.

Section one focuses primarily on the history of the prudence standard tracing back to 1830; its restatement to include "be observed by a prudent man dealing with the property of another" to the 1974 ERISA "what a person with like aims under like circumstances" would do.

It does give us an objective versus subjective standard. A prudent trustee behaves as other trustees in a similar situation would behave. Sections 2-9 of the Act identify the factors that bear on prudent investor behavior.

Section Two is considered the heart of the Act; the meat of the matter, as it were. It deals with **Standard of Care; Portfolio Strategy; Risk and Return Objectives.**

a) *A trustee shall invest and manage trust assets as a prudent investor would, by considering the purposes, terms, distribution requirements, and other circumstances of the trust. In satisfying this standard the trustee shall exercise reasonable care, skill and caution.*

b) *Considering the purposes, terms, distribution requirements and other circumstances of the trust.*

These are the sentences that matter the most to us here and throughout this narrative. In a "normal" trust you would have to consider provisions to create income for the beneficiaries; conditions under which the current beneficiaries can invade principal; the tax regime of the trust assets themselves; as well as the tax situation of the beneficiaries. Since some of your assets may be in IRAs you may have actual distribution requirements; but regardless, one of the purposes of this trust will be to provide you with income for your lifetime (which may be a long time indeed). Only after those requirements are "funded" should you be TOO concerned about the remainder beneficiaries (your heirs). You need to create quality language in the event you die before you spend the trust assets, but your first duty as trustee is to yourself. Many of the "terms" of the trust we are discussing are your personalities, skills and fears, as we have explored previously. The theme is sounded again in this, the first paragraph of the Act's core section.

c) A trustee's investment and management decisions respecting individual assets must be evaluated not in isolation but in the context of the trust portfolio as a whole and as part of an overall investment strategy having risk and return objectives reasonably suited to the trust.

When investing in equities our overall investment strategy involves creating an efficient portfolio based on asset classes. We sell the asset classes that have appreciated in relation to the balance of the asset classes, and buy the asset classes that under-performed in relationship to the balance of the asset classes. When the market eventually adjusts and the under-performing asset class becomes the over-performing asset class, we sell the shares we bought "on the cheap" in order to buy whatever asset classes went down. If we looked at investments in isolation we would have had a very hard time selling the large growth, technology related assets in the late 1990s because they had performed so well in the recent past. We also would have had a hard time shifting to value, foreign or whatever other asset classes we bought at the time because recent history said they under-performed. It is the performance of the whole and how holding one asset class affects the efficiency of the portfolio that matters. It is not an emotional thing.

If we create a solid plan and identify our trust's constitution we can help reduce or eliminate emotion in the areas of the trust that are not directly related to equities. Creating effective income plans requires us to look at the various ways we can access income and their overall effect on our taxation on the value of trust assets. This means we do not look at the ways we *receive* our income in isolation, either. In any given year in any given trust there is a most effective way to access income. What is it in your case? Work on it. Once again it is a paramount controllable item in *your* trust's management.

d) **Among the circumstances that a trustee shall consider in investing and managing trust assets are such of the following as are relevant to the trust or its beneficiaries:**

   (1) General economic conditions;

   (2) The possible effects of inflation or deflation;

   (3) The expected tax consequences of investment decisions or strategies;

   (4) The role that each asset or course of action plays within the overall trust portfolio, which may include financial assets, interests in closely held enterprises, tangible and intangible personal property, and real property;

   (5) The expected total return from income and appreciation of capital;

   (6) Other resources of the beneficiaries;

   (7) Needs for liquidity, regularity of income, and preservation of capital, and;

   (8) An asset's special relationship or special value, if any, to the purposes of the trust or to one or more beneficiaries.

This spells out what we have been talking about all along. Look specifically at items 3, 4, 6, 7 & 8. ALL trust assets -- sentimental, situational, emotional or otherwise. One of the driving reasons for writing this type of explanation of the Act is that I cannot accept the delegation of all trust responsibilities (serve as the financial advisor) for as many people as I would like. As a third party advisor we accept the delegation of the equities management function from fiduciaries of various pensions and charities, trust companies and actual trusts. This limited delegation makes me uncomfortable because the nature of those sorts of relationships is such where the balance of the information regarding you, your trust, the important stuff, is left untouched. One of the citadel assets of our firm is that we do no harm. Maybe you should not even be investing in a 401(k) that we manage; perhaps that money would be better directed to other trust investments. Maybe you should be funding it more due to tax consequences in your life. Since there is no way for me to know, it seemed incumbent on me to share these fundamental truths with you and, potentially, your advisors. If you have an advisor, get them into the entirety of your trust; YOUR planning. You will soon discover if they are capable of (or if their business model allows for) accepting that sort of delegation.

e) *A trustee shall make a reasonable effort to verify facts relevant to the investment and management of trust assets.*

Two comments regarding this subsection: If you are the trustee, you need to create this evaluation. If you have a financial advisor, stockbroker, insurance salesman, whatever, they need to develop a pretty in-depth understanding of who you are and what you bring to the table if they are to be effective. Not nearly enough advisors are, or consider themselves, fiduciaries for their clients. You have to create a course of action for the beneficiary that is prudent and suitable in light of all of the assets of the trust, whatever they may be.

Secondly, I tend to separate the management of the equities portfolio from the balance of the trust's assets in this context because "the relevant facts" becomes a monster that will not obey. It is separate, with the exception of taxes created by the process of maintaining a balanced portfolio, which we must always consider.

f) *A trustee may invest in any kind of property or type of investment consistent with the standards of this Act.*

What does "consistent with the standards of this Act" mean? *A prudent Trustee acts as other prudent trustees would act under the same circumstances* from section one. Anything may be suitable under some circumstances and unsuitable under other circumstances.

g) *A trustee who has special skills and expertise, or is named trustee in reliance upon the trustee's representation that the trustee has special skills or expertise, has a duty to use those special skills or expertise.*

I feel this provision is here to make sure that if a trustee or an agent has skills they MUST employ them. It is implied that they will. In the Act, it is explicit that they will. Are you the trustee of your trust? Are you using all of your expertise to benefit your trust?

The balance of section two deals with restating the objective standard applied in section one. It addresses the portfolio standard, which refers back to using all assets and all trust circumstances in making decisions. The discussion on Risk and Return on page 10 of the Act is the first place the risk versus return curve, or efficient frontier, is mentioned in the Act.

This seems like a reasonable place to attempt to explain MPT in understandable terms. We have created a DVD, which you can acquire, that may do a better job than the more one-dimensional effort I can create with the written word. If you have seen and understand it, skip forward to "Back to the ACT" starting on page 37.

MODERN PORTFOLIO THEORY

A graduate student named Harry Markowitz discovered Modern Portfolio Theory in 1950. Markowitz and his associates studied the subject and wrote additional papers in support of the theory until he (and some of his contemporaries) was awarded the Nobel Prize in economics in 1990. From the years of study by Markowitz and others, the financial community has come to accept many of their findings as established truths. So much so that references to it, and implicit recommendations for its use, are abundant in this Act and the concepts of the prudent investor standard.

What Markowitz discovered is that there is a way you could blend your equity investments that would cause you to receive the highest possible return based on the risk you are willing to take. This was unheard of in 1950 and unfortunately is still extremely under-utilized even today.

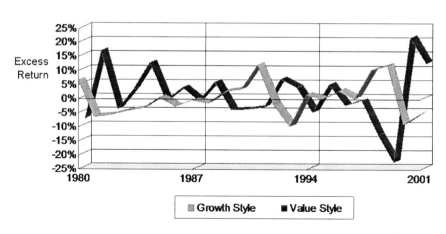

Figure 2

Let's begin with the accepted truths. **Figure 2** illustrates the variance of returns if you compare the returns of asset classes considered to be either value or growth. The accepted concept is that certain assets do not correlate to one another; in economics jargon they are co-variant. They vary differently. We understand that large cap growth behaves differently than small cap value. So some asset classes are going up in market value while others are going down, or they are going up or down at different rates of speed.

Diversification from Combining Investments

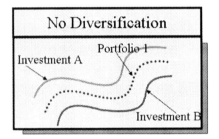

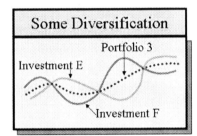

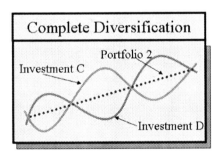

Figure 3

Figure 3 demonstrates the effects of simple diversification. Blending two investments that behave differently allows you to smooth your ride and potentially receive higher returns. But those are the basics of diversification.

Markowitz and his fellow number crunchers also made another discovery that advisors know but seem to forget, and evidence shows the individual investors seem to have missed all together.

As **Figure 4** shows, over 90% of the deviation (which translates into return) of your or any portfolio is determined by the blend of the asset classes rather than factors such as timing or selection. What that means is that buying the ABC fund instead of the XYZ fund means almost nothing. It is the blend of asset CLASSES taken in combination with all other asset classes in the portfolio that will create the return.

This rejects the buy and hold strategy out of hand if you are using mutual funds or separate accounts to create your pooled diversification.

Modern Portfolio Theory goes a few steps further than the discovery that the blend of assets creates the result. It determines which blend of assets to use to facilitate the best result based on the risk you are intending to take.

MPT uses as its measure of risk the analysis of standard deviation. Standard deviation is the measure of how much something will be different, or deviate from, the expected result. If you have a deviation of 10% and an expected return of 9%, you should expect that over time you will receive between 8.1% to 9.9%, or a 10% swing from the expected return.

Once you create a portfolio with the proper blend, you manage asset classes to maintain that blend. It is the process of doing this that seems to make the theory extremely effective.

What Drives Portfolio Performance

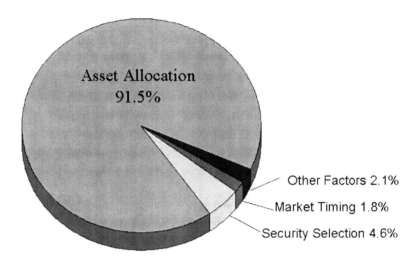

Asset Allocation
91.5%

Other Factors 2.1%

Market Timing 1.8%

Security Selection 4.6%

Figure 4

Figure 5 shows the efficient frontier and three portfolios. When you already have an inefficient portfolio as shown in Figure 5, you have two options. First, reduce the risk of the portfolio to match the potential return, or change the return of the portfolio to match the risk you have already undertaken. Seems reasonable.

If you are starting from scratch you need to assess the risk you are willing to take, and build a portfolio that is as efficient as possible based on that risk. We use a relatively simple system to help people think through this. (It is included at the end of this section, page 33) In our case our creation of a risk tolerance focuses on how, and when, the portfolio is going to be accessed for income. We focus our risk management on income planning. There is an exception to this rule worth noting. If you are active in creating a real estate portfolio, your ability to intelligently acquire and manage debt is arguably your biggest asset. Whatever your normal risk tolerance is will likely be reduced by the importance of maintaining principal levels over all near term horizons. Why? Lenders consider your equities as assets and if you are aggressively invested and lose 30% in a year, it may take you out of position to create your next debt and your next acquisition. All other factors could indicate your ability to work through that one-year loss in search of the long-term gain, but they would not take the entire trust into account. In other words, your personal ability to create wealth outside the equities portfolio has a major impact on how much risk you take within your equities portfolio, particularly when considering debt acquisition.

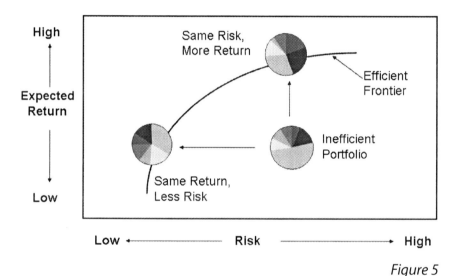

Figure 5

Let's say we established how much risk we are going to take. How do we proceed? We diversify the portfolio to cause it to land on the efficient frontier. We use software called Frontier Analytics to do the math necessary to formulate the blend. The inputs we use for the formula are dollars worth of specific asset classes. There are essentially 18 different asset classes to choose from; our firm uses 14 of those classes to create a portfolio. In Figure 5 you see three portfolios with different asset classes populating each of the "pies." You can see that the composition of the portfolio changed in an effort to make the portfolio more efficient. Pretend that the efficient portfolio was your starting point. Every day the market conditions change. Over the course of many days the composition of the pie changes because, as we learned before, different asset classes go up and down at different rates, so the portfolio has to change. The asset classes that did well in relation to the others expanded their portion of the pie, whereas the under-performing asset class portions of the pie were reduced. What does MPT tell us to do under those circumstances? We are to sell that asset class that went up and purchase the asset class that went down. This is the act that causes MPT to be so effective. It seems simple but it's precisely opposite of how most folks view investing. This is an exercise of selling high and buying low, not an attempt to buy low and sell high. Usually people talk about buying an asset low and selling it high. The problem is, on an individual stock, mutual fund or asset class, how can you know when low is low enough to buy and high is high enough to sell? You can't. So emotions, fear and/or greed drive the decision making progress. You can, however, know when something is high in relative terms to the balance of the asset classes you own. The composition of your pie tells you so.

Figure 6 is actually a series of figures attempting to illustrate how MPT harvests the fluctuations of the market. You begin with a simple portfolio of two asset classes; we will consider one growth and the other value to simplify the illustration. They begin at equal prices and values. One asset goes up 10% and the other goes down 10%. If you got a statement at this time, it would look like the market was flat as far as you were concerned; your account value would not have changed.

HARVESTING MARKET FLUCTUATIONS

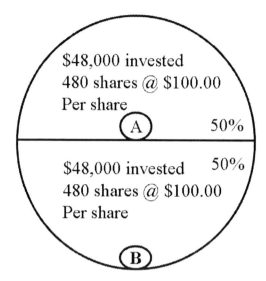

$48,000 invested
480 shares @ $100.00
Per share

A   50%

$48,000 invested   50%
480 shares @ $100.00
Per share

B

Figure 6a

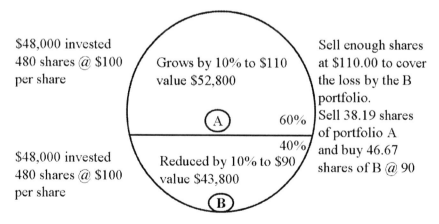

$48,000 invested
480 shares @ $100
per share

Grows by 10% to $110
value $52,800

A   60%

40%

$48,000 invested
480 shares @ $100
per share

Reduced by 10% to $90
value $43,800

B

Sell enough shares
at $110.00 to cover
the loss by the B
portfolio.
Sell 38.19 shares
of portfolio A
and buy 46.67
shares of B @ 90

Figure 6b

Harvesting Market Fluctuations

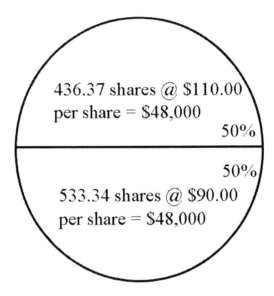

436.37 shares @ $110.00
per share = $48,000

50%

50%

533.34 shares @ $90.00
per share = $48,000

Figure 6c

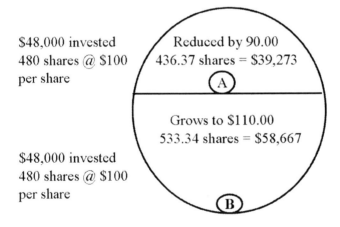

$48,000 invested
480 shares @ $100
per share

Reduced by 90.00
436.37 shares = $39,273

Ⓐ

Grows to $110.00
533.34 shares = $58,667

$48,000 invested
480 shares @ $100
per share

Ⓑ

New Value $97,940 , a 1.98% increase on seemingly negating actions

Figure 6d

FIGURES 6A, B, C AND D

We then sell the required number of shares of the asset class that went up, and purchase the amount of shares of the asset class that went down, in order to rebalance the portfolio. (Note that you sold less shares to acquire more.) The next step shows the market reversing direction (Figure 7 is a table of how various asset classes rank over a period of years and demonstrates that they move around some). The asset class we own fewer shares of goes back down and the asset class we own more shares of goes back up. If you had not sold what went up and bought what went down you would have received a statement that once again looked like the market was flat as far as you were concerned; your account value had not changed.

BUT, if you had harvested those fluctuations, you would have made a profit in a "flat or choppy" market. MPT does this harvesting on a macro basis, taking all of the asset classes into account.

Another enormous consideration is the behavior of the fund managers. We subscribe to a service called Investment View, which tells us which asset classes each mutual fund owns and in what proportions, and provides return information and rankings of each fund in relation to its peers. A quick note on rankings ("stars" or happy faces); these rankings are difficult to rely on for several reasons, but the largest one is style drift. A ranking service (Investment View is not really one) places a fund in a sector or style box and rates it in relation to other funds in that sector or style box. The problem is the fund is often not invested heavily in the style in which it is "placed." A fund that calls itself "Growth Domestic" in Investment View and is described as large cap growth by the big ranking firm, holds roughly a third of its assets in domestic growth of any kind, at the time of this writing, and has just about 9% invested in large cap growth. When an institutional manager uses this fund as its large growth fund, just what are you getting? The bottom line of all of this is that you need to know what each fund owns by percentage of asset class, and those percentages change all the time. We get updated reports on all of the funds monthly and do reallocations on a quarterly basis unless there has been a radical change in either market conditions or the holdings within the asset classes of our core funds.

Figures 7

I realize that this can get a bit deep. The basic reality is that there are multiple forces at work changing the constitution and efficiency of your portfolio. The role of the manager is to maintain your standard deviation in a way that is most consistent with the selling-high and buying-low process.

If you have been paying attention you may have just had an "ah-ha" moment. All of this sounded so good, but what about this fund manager style changing my portfolio? This is the crack in the armor of MPT as it relates to funds. In a perfect world the only variable that we would manage would be market fluctuations, but we are not in a perfect world and it is impossible to maintain a portfolio that is exclusively managed by the sell-high-buy-low process. This is the truth. There is an imperfection in execution. We can end up with the correct balance on a quarterly basis but we cannot be sure the manager sold his or her assets high to get us there. Without creating a portfolio with hundreds of individual securities and enormous taxes in the process of reallocation, you cannot execute MPT with pristine perfection. You can only get close and maintain your inconsistency. But you CAN create correctly-allocated portfolios periodically; in our company's case, every 90 days or so. The UPIA seems to say we ought to reallocate at least annually. But in our case, particularly in light of style drift, more frequency is preferred.

Modern Portfolio Theory is the most accepted method of managing money available, yet most professionals do not implement it. This leads us to wonder why. There are other Third Party Managers that talk about doing a form of MPT but they "tweak" or "enhance" it. If you haven't discovered this up until now, remember this: You cannot tweak or modify MPT;

Stock Performance

Best →	1994	1995	1996	1997	1998	1999	2000	2001	2002	2003	2004 → Worst
	Foreign Stocks 8.06%	Large Growth Stocks 38.13%	REITs 35.75%	Large Growth Stocks 36.53%	Large Growth Stocks 42.16%	Small Growth Stocks 43.09%	REITs 25.88%	REITs 15.50%	Inv-Grade Bonds 10.27%	Small Growth Stocks 48.54%	REITs 30.41%
	Large Growth Stocks 3.13%	Large Value Stocks 36.99%	Large Growth Stocks 23.96%	Mid-Cap Stocks 32.26%	Foreign Stocks 20.33%	Large Growth Stocks 28.25%	Small Value Stocks 22.83%	Small Value Stocks 14.03%	REITs 5.22%	Small Value Stocks 46.03%	Small Value Stocks 22.25%
	REITs 0.81%	Small Growth Stocks 31.04%	Large Value Stocks 21.99%	Small Value Stocks 31.78%	Foreign Stocks 19.12%	Foreign Stocks 27.30%	Mid-Cap Stocks 17.51%	Inv-Grade Bonds 8.42%	High Yield Bonds -1.37%	Foreign Stocks 39.17%	Foreign Stocks 20.70%
	Large Value Stocks -0.64%	Mid-Cap Stocks 30.94%	Small Value Stocks 21.37%	Large Value Stocks 29.98%	Large Value Stocks 14.67%	Mid-Cap Stocks 14.72%	Inv-Grade Bonds 11.63%	High Yield Bonds 5.28%	Small Value Stocks -11.43%	REITs 38.47%	Mid-Cap Stocks 16.48%
	High Yield Bonds -1.01%	High Yield Bonds 19.17%	Mid-Cap Stocks 19.20%	REITs 18.87%	Inv-Grade Bonds 8.67%	Large Value Stocks 12.72%	Large Value Stocks 6.08%	Mid-Cap Stocks -0.61%	Mid-Cap Stocks -14.51%	Mid-Cap Stocks 35.61%	Large Value Stocks 15.71%
	Small Value Stocks -1.55%	Inv-Grade Bonds 18.48%	High Yield Bonds 11.35%	Small Growth Stocks 12.95%	High Yield Bonds 1.87%	High Yield Bonds 2.39%	High Yield Bonds -5.86%	Small Growth Stocks -9.23%	Foreign Stocks -15.66%	Large Value Stocks 31.79%	Small Growth Stocks 14.31%
	Small Growth Stocks -2.43%	REITs 18.31%	Small Growth Stocks 11.26%	High Yield Bonds 12.77%	Small Growth Stocks 1.23%	Inv-Grade Bonds 0.82%	Foreign Stocks -13.96%	Large Value Stocks -11.71%	Large Value Stocks -30.15%	High Yield Bonds 28.96%	High Yield Bonds 11.14%
	Inv-Grade Bonds 2.92%	Foreign Stocks 11.55%	Foreign Stocks 6.36%	Inv-Grade Bonds 9.68%	Small Value Stocks -6.45%	Small Value Stocks -1.49%	Large Growth Stocks -22.08%	Large Growth Stocks -12.73%	Large Growth Stocks -23.59%	Large Growth Stocks 25.67%	Large Growth Stocks 6.13%
	Mid-Cap Stocks -3.57%		Inv-Grade Bonds 3.61%	Foreign Stocks 2.06%	REITs -18.82%	REITs -6.48%	Small Growth Stocks -22.43%	Foreign Stocks -21.21%	Small Growth Stocks -30.26%	Inv-Grade Bonds 4.11%	Inv-Grade Bonds 4.34%

Figure 7

31

you can only implement it. The moment you seek to enhance the theory you have stopped implementing it. Oh, you could and should choose better than average funds to create your asset blends, but that is the extent of your ability to affect the outcome. As noted in Figure 3, very little of the result will be affected by those choices. People are averse to selling on the way up because they want to participate in "momentum," but they forget there are two sides to the equation. What are we not buying at the right relative price while we guess how long an asset class will run? Therein lies the problem.

My theory (and that is all it is) as to why it is not used widely has three components. First, where it is simple to understand it is not easy to implement. It requires a dedicated infrastructure and a fair amount of time to do. It is not readily "automated." Second, the theory does not allow you to add value in addition to implementation, as if that wasn't value enough, and large companies cannot or will not "sell" it. A friend of mine claims it lacks sizzle. That's okay; I prefer steak. Lastly, it was the time it came of age. Where the financial services community started paying attention to MPT in the late 1980's, it was not until after the UPIA that financial professionals began attempting to implement it. This was is the mid to late 1990's and if you look at the table in Figure 7, what was dominating the top of the market at the time? Large growth. The major indices that were being reported at the time were the DOW and the S&P (that has changed to Dow and NASDAQ for the time being). The practice of MPT does not compete well with those conditions. We were selling the assets that were going up and buying the ones that went down. Where we "made" money, we under-performed what the public's perception of the benchmark was. Now, after the market reversed and we owned all those asset classes that were relatively inexpensive at the time we bought them, we started looking pretty smart. By that time professionals had abandoned MPT in an effort to "beat the market" and/or win or retain clients, which for you, the consumer, was a bad thing. I know of few of us who stuck to and have stayed stuck to the discipline over the years. MPT is not a short-term strategy; Sell high, buy low and repeat until death.

RISK STRATAS

Creative Wealth Strategies creates portfolios within variable annuities and qualified plans focused around three stratas of risk, based on the client's use of the money and attitudes toward risk. We do not have a weighted "risk tolerance" questionnaire that is supposed to determine the client's risk. In every questionnaire I have seen or worked with there is a high level of subjectivity to how the questions are answered and/or scored.

We ask the financial advisor to work with the client to determine the eventual use of the assets. They need to develop an understanding of how each asset will be affected by other assets, income sources and guarantees, or the lack thereof, to determine which portfolio makes the most sense for the client.

First, there are three terms to define:

GIB: *a*"guaranteed income benefit," usually requiring annuitization

GWB: *a* "guaranteed withdrawal benefit;" an option usually not requiring annuitization

Standard Deviation: The formula for how much something deviates from expected results. A quantitative rather than economic, or benchmark-oriented measure.

Our portfolios are designed in three groups:

Risk One is for clients who are using a portion of the income invested now, or are likely to utilize it in the next 10 years. This portfolio seems best suited to people with two widely different risk profiles. One for those who do not like risk and would be out of the market if not for a GIB, and one for those who are relatively comfortable with market gyrations and are not GIB or GWB candidates, but want a smooth ride.

Our average standard deviation for this group of portfolios is 10.58.

Risk Two is for clients who are either postponing accessing income from this investment for 10 or more years or are using it for income on a very limited (1%-3%) basis. This is excellent for people who have an income guarantee that they are willing to use but are still uncomfortable with too much volatility. They would use the income benefit but would much rather try to ride out the losses through systematic withdrawals.

Long-term investors who choose not to use riders will find this a bit more profitable than Risk One, and generally a little less expensive to run.

Our average standard deviation for this group of portfolios is 11.90%.

Risk Three is intended to be used with long-term investments that will not be accessed within the first 10 to 15 years and are unlikely to be exhausted over the next 20 years. We use this for the third and fourth layer of an income plan, in conjunction with "high water mark" options for income benefits one would exercise in 15 years, or assets that have a death benefit but MAY be used as income in the event of unforeseen circumstances. Often we cluster a half dozen smaller portfolios of this risk type for clients to access principal upon withdrawal to cover future, if yet undefined, expenses.

Our average standard deviation for this group of portfolios is 13.19%.

You could and should rightly wonder why we do not have a standard deviation and expected return that is lower than our Risk One portfolio. The reason is two-fold. First, when you get down below an 8% expected long-range goal it is easy to question why one is in the market in the first place. And, if the need is short term, a client probably should not be in the market at all. Second, and more importantly, when mutual funds or separate accounts are used to complete the allocation; we would be using a large portion of our allocation in Bond Funds. Bond Fund managers, by their nature, are in and out of positions all the time. One month a total return fund might have 70% in corporate assets, the next month 5%. Their cash accounts fluctuate wildly and once you have a bunch of cash in your portfolio, all you can say for sure is that by the time you receive your next report, the cash may have moved, but to which Asset class? That we do not know. Interestingly, as we sought to actually *implement* MPT, we found that unless you are using individual holdings, taking less risk on the efficient frontier caused us to create more risk within the portfolio due to manager drift and short-term yield curve swings.

The reason we do not go farther out on the risk curve is also two-fold. First, we lose efficiency. We get to a place where we have to take 10% more risk to get 1% more return. It makes little sense. If you have someone who is trying to hit a home run, or is in the unfortunate circumstance where they are trying to establish a high-water mark death benefit quickly, you can usually build a portfolio of sector, specialty or index funds and shoot for the moon without the drag of our fees on the death benefit, **and** usually at a lower internal cost than we seek to deliver.

We could have built several portfolios between the deviations to appear to have more offerings, but saw no value in it. We try to emphasize and re-emphasize that it is the income planning, the management of taxes and the timing of accessing assets that will most dramatically affect clients' results. Our job as advisors is simply to help them establish a plan, with risk and return management as one component of the plan, and implement it as effectively as possible. One percent more or less in establishing deviation is going to have little effect on the outcome.

Averages were created by adding up the deviations of our portfolios and dividing by the number of portfolios in question, as opposed to an average based on account values.

BACK TO THE ACT

Continuing on page 10 of the Act are factors affecting investment. Not surprisingly, the focus is on taxes. Taxes at death, taxes of the beneficiaries, taxes of the trust in its entirety, and, specifically, taxes created in portfolio management. All of these are aspects of total trust management, including a last item mentioning the personal considerations of the beneficiaries and emotional attachment to certain assets.

The duty to monitor embraces management. MPT fulfills the duty to monitor within the equities arena. You are in charge of monitoring your program to see if you are on track with your goals, staying within your constitutional boundaries, and determining if you are effectively controlling those things you can control; primarily taxes and your level of commitment.

The last component of section two deals with the duty to investigate and a now-redundant discourse on how all assets are potentially suitable and all aspects of the trust must be considered. It also deals with professional fiduciaries and the distinction of the application of the prudent investor standard. It seems that the standard is relational; the standard for amateurs is the standard of prudent amateurs, and the standard for professionals is the standard for prudent professionals. Doesn't it stand to reason you would want the professional standard to apply in as many areas of your trust's life as possible?

Sections 3-8 of the Uniform Prudent Investor Act essentially support the concept of using the techniques employed by MPT and pooling your assets. Pooling, in this case, meaning using mutual funds and variable annuity sub-accounts. Review them when you finish reading these next few pages. I just don't want to cover the same ground we covered in exploring how MPT works.

The last of the Act's sections, section 9, deals with matters of delegation. This is important for a few reasons as it relates to us as people, as opposed to simply our equities investments. We tend to avoid financial advisors, loan originators, car salesmen

anyone who gets compensated for helping us buy things
:cause we presume they are not looking out for our best
ııterests. In this Act it states we have a duty to investigate and
we NEED to do so, but after we investigate we, in many cases,
need to delegate.

You can purchase the software and subscribe to the services
that will enable you to create effective portfolios, and you could
certainly learn how, but unless you are worth several million
dollars and love to play with this kind of thing it would not be
cost effective to do so. If you have the resources, love to play
with the numbers and stick to the discipline, you should perform
as well as I do because MPT is MPT and I cannot enhance the
result beyond that. You would save my fee and possibly enjoy
it. Possibly not.

Tax management individuals and **good** loan originators ought
to pay for themselves over time, and with the right financial
constitution **you** are the best suited to create a plan for wealth
creation. If you have already created a fair bit of wealth it
may make sense to hire someone to manage the entire trust
portfolio, if you can find someone who will take the entire trust
into account and has the skills to manage the outcomes. You
will recognize whether or not an advisor has these skills after a
couple of appointments by the direction of the meeting. If he
or she is focusing on your skills, your wills and trusts as well your
non-equities potential, you are probably in the right place.

It may be good to look for professional designations when
seeking an advisor. Designations do not, by themselves, mean
your advisor has diverse experiences, but it is a place start
when filtering whom your advisor should be. The professional
designation CFP or Certified Financial Planner is the entry level,
or easiest designation to earn. A step up from that is a CLU or
Chartered Life Underwriter who has learned, if not applied, a
great deal of advance estate and financial planning concepts
as part of his or her education. A step above that is ChFC or
Chartered Financial Consultant. Those are the "big three" as
far as designations go. After that you get into specialties. For

instance, one of my designations is the AEP or Accredited Estate Planner. It's part of a master's degree in Financial Services (MSFS) but is focused on Estate Planning and Estate Tax Avoidance.

All of that said, I know a handful of un-credentialed planners who are very competent and handful of credentialed advisors who are very incompetent. So the designations, or lack thereof, should not be the driving factor. Experience is very important, but not necessarily in terms of years. I know many people who have had the same one-year of experience repeated 20 times. If you are an entrepreneur, hire an advisor who is also an entrepreneur. If you are a real estate investor, try to find an advisor who not only agrees with the idea, but has done it themselves and/or has experience in developing individual real estate portfolios.

INCOME PLANNING

The UPIA has a great number of references to income planning in indirect ways. The constant reference to taking all trust circumstances into account as well as those of the beneficiaries sings the same song as creating effective income plans.

The first rule in creating effective income plans is to generate multiple tax platforms to work with. The more tax regimes we have to manage the better off we are. That means we should purchase assets that create current deductions when possible. 401(k) plans are a step in that direction but should be augmented with real estate if you can handle the effort. After the current deductible options are explored, look at assets that create current and eventual tax efficiency; variable annuities, Roth 401(k) plans, even life insurance if you are young enough and build it correctly, are excellent assets to access on a tax favorable, or at least controllable, basis. Even cash can be a very suitable investment for near term income needs if you are controlling taxation.

Here is an example. Pretend you can live on $50,000 per year and your collective social security is $25,000. Withdraw $85,000 from your IRA and pay your taxes. You will pay tax on 85% of your $25,000 social security, making $21,250 taxable. At 20% you would pay $4,250 in taxes in year one. In years two and three you withdraw the cash from the bank (which is paying you 3% or so) and live on it. It is likely you would pay zero tax on social security in years 2 and 3.

If you withdrew $30,000 from your IRA every year to live on instead, you would likely pay the $4,250 of tax on the SSI every year. This act of taking one larger withdrawal up front would cause you to pay a slightly higher rate in that year, but when stacked up against the $8,500 tax savings in the withdrawal technique, the effects are minimal. _And,_ for the two years you have little to no income, your tax rate goes down, which increases your ability to access lower brackets on "other" taxable transactions.

This is a simple, straightforward example. Let's look at something a little more esoteric. You're an X-year-old couple with $300,000 in an IRA and $300,000 in mutual funds. You are planning to retire in five years. You will continue to save in both accounts, as your kids are finally on their own.

Consider purchasing a series of variable annuities using the mutual fund investments in your name and in the name of your spouse. Three each ought to do it for a total of six variable annuities. It is important that those contracts be with at least three different companies (the IRS says purchasing more than one VA in the same company by the same taxpayer in the same year will cause them to be taxed together... they understood this idea, the son of a guns). Purchase from three firms for him, and a matching three for her. I know that the financial pornography says that variable annuities are expensive and therefore bad. I am not going to go through all the information to support my ideas but will cut to the bottom line. Based on performance and flexibility, variable annuities are more suitable more often than mutual funds. The pundits tend to argue that the price and compensation are too high. I am not interested in the price, but the cost, and I find Variable Annuities beyond competitive. I think I get paid .5% to 2% more when I help you purchase one in relation to a mutual fund. Hardly enough to sell your soul for AND you rarely replace one VA for another. Have you ever heard of anyone replacing one mutual fund for another? Ca-Ching. Plus, as you follow the MPT process you are selling high and buying low, which often creates taxation in mutual funds, and selling slivers of mutual funds of different fund families almost invariably creates some sort of transaction fee.

If you don't know, a variable annuity is essentially a tax-deferred shell that holds a bunch of selected mutual-fund-like separate accounts. In this example the tax deferral and eventual access are the keys.

If you put $50,000 in each of these six contracts you will ˈ have a tax basis of $50,000 each. Make maximum contr into your IRA/401(k) and reduce your debt over the nˈ years. Create one to two years worth of cash (instead of ɩnutual funds) before you get to retirement so that you can use that cash as a tax management tool (it will also reduce the risk of starting distributions during poor market conditions.). In year one of retirement you have six accounts worth roughly $70,000 each. You have invested them with different risks so some will be higher, others lower, but it illustrates the concept. In year one of retirement you take $20,000 of ordinary income from one of the annuities (as much as is tax intelligent) and the balance of your income from Social Security and/or cash (as little as is tax intelligent). The next year you can dip into the first annuity to get tax-free return of principal even as you skim taxable income off the top of the other annuities. You end up in a situation where you can intelligently manage the tax tiers of the group of annuity contracts in concert with your other assets. Mutual funds do not offer that kind of control. Plus, as you manage them using MPT you tend to create ordinary income, which is tax inefficient. So often my choice when using mutual funds is to be inefficient within the scope of MPT or inefficient within the scope of UPIA. This illustrates another reason the pundits drive me nuts with the rhetoric. It is clear most have never had to actually implement anything!

If you are a high-income earner/high taxpayer, consider acquiring a handful of income properties in an effort to create tax deductions currently, and the potential to access monies from those investments in a number of tax-efficient ways in the future.

I am fond of saying "Once you have the assets you have the options," and when income planning, maximizing your tax management options is to the character of wealth management as carbon is to steel.

There are as many variations on asset creation and income accessibility as there are people attempting to implement them. I hope to have inspired you to make the most of yours.

If you choose to begin this journey there are some books you should read. I have a "Fundamental Five," but there are many more that might be more digestible if you have not been reading "success books" over the years.

MY FIVE:

The Magic of Thinking Big, *David J Schwartz PHD*

Acres of Diamonds, *Russell H Conwell*

Think and Grow Rich, *Napoleon Hill*

The Master Key to Riches, *Napoleon Hill*

The Greatest Secret in the World, *Og Mandino*

The first two are lay ups but the last three are pretty intense efforts to study. These are some more I would consider in no particular order:

How to Win Friends and Influence People, *Dale Carnegie*

How to Stop Worrying and Start Living, *Dale Carnegie*

The Go Getter, *Peter B Kyne*

How I Raised Myself From Failure to Success Through Selling, *Frank Betger*

The Autobiography of Benjamin Franklin,

Rich Dad Poor Dad, *Robert Kiyosaki*

Retire Rich, Retire Young, *Robert Kiyosaki*

Cash Flow Quadrant, *Robert Kiyosaki*

Who Moved My Cheese? , *Spencer Johnson*

Seven Habits of Highly Effective People, *Steven Covey*

The Eighth Habit, *Steven Covey*

The Prayer of Jabez, *Bruce Wilkinson*

How to Run Your Business So You Can Leave It In Style, *John Brown*

The Millionaire Next Door, *Thomas Stanley*

Hung By The Tongue, *Francis Martin*

The World is Flat, *Thomas Friedman*

PROGRAMS:

The ultimate goals program*Bryan Tracy*

Tax Strategies for Small Business*Sandy Botkin*

Tax Strategies for Real Estate*Sandy Botkin*

I have a bit of advice to my clients regarding the book Think and Grow Rich. It is the mother of all improvement books. My clients are asked to read it once a year until I tell them to stop. If you never picked up this or any other book again, the tools in that book, though difficult to digest, will take you anywhere you want to go.

WEALTH AND INCOME CREATION:

If you are in active income-creation mode, Inertia and its employment are of fundamental importance. This is a chapter that was written some time ago and applies directly to the creation of wealth. If you are more interested in creating wills and trusts and avoiding taxes on the wealth you have already created, you may want to skip Ancillary Business Activities and Who Do You Know Who?, but I would take the time to read the following Inertia chapter. It has had a wonderful impact on many of my clients, however they are situated.

INERTIA

My son was working on his science homework the other day and there was a multiple-choice question regarding inertia. Interestingly, none of the answers were right on point so we had to choose the least wrong answer, much like decisions we make everyday. The concept of inertia is essentially that an object in motion remains in motion until an equal or opposite force is applied against it. If you roll a ball on a flat surface it will roll until friction and gravity stop it.

I got to thinking about my businesses and financial plans and those of my clients, and decided that inertia is a key to success in any undertaking. An object at rest remains at rest. Any idea or process un-begun will never get done. Anything started carries with it its own momentum and creates actions, activities or decisions as it rolls along. Each action and decision keeps the ball moving along – sometimes with little effort, sometimes with Herculean effort – but it moves along nonetheless. Perhaps it is one of the reasons certain people get an inordinate amount accomplished and often do not seem ridiculously harried in the process.

I have often referred to my personal and business life as an effort to keep an ever-increasing amount of plates spinning. A better analogy is that we are developing an ever-increasing amount of positive inertia. It may not always feel that way, but it's certainly a far better way to frame it if we want to use it to our advantage. How can we use this natural law to our benefit, to channel its power into your life and mine? One step is to recognize it. Upon reflection you will likely see patterns in your life where you created a certain activity and the activity took on a life of its own, good or bad. One thing leads to another and eventually one of three things occur. The project or process is completed, if it is a project that has an end, or you create

47

infrastructure and systems to manage and integrate the new activity into your daily existence (like a good exercise program, for instance). Or, after the initial enthusiasm has worn off, friction and gravity cause the activity, goal, project, exercise regime, to die an uncompleted or unfulfilled death.

A few keys will help insure our success in developing positive inertia in our financial and business lives:

Be selective about the things you start. We can only manage so much momentum at any one time. We can increase our capacity, but there is still a capacity that we reach. Wherever we are on the curve as far as our ability to manage the big mo is where we must begin to expand it, whether we are self employed or Microsoft Corporation. But don't waste energy and positive momentum by creating projects that are unlikely to be completed. There is another natural law at work here; that any one of your activities that creates friction and negative momentum affects all of the activities and projects that are in your world. That may seem obvious as you read it, but few people bring that idea to consciousness.

If you look at all of your activities, projects or financial practices, would you find any that are contrary to your stated objectives? If so, can you systematize or change them to make them consistent with your stated objectives? If you cannot or will not, why are you doing them?

There is a concept referred to as zero-based thinking; if there is anything in your life you would not do over, get out of it as efficiently and expediently as possible. The best way to do that is to be critical and think through those things that will utilize valuable time and financial resources *before* you enter into them. This is almost always less expensive than stopping momentum on a wayward project, because an equal and opposite force is needed to end a project once it has begun. It's like throwing out a light anchor on your ship. If you throw out enough, the whole ship stops. Even one or two, thrown to the side, will change the direction of your ship, sometimes so subtly you do not realize it until you are well off course.

Start the things you select. Create an action plan and implement strategies in your financial life. Understand that nothing is perfect or guaranteed. The only thing we can say with certainty is that 20 years from now we will look at decisions made today and say, "I would have done better if…" We just can't let the "if" be "I would have done SOMETHING." Once you start planning, momentum develops. Once you begin to implement, actions and decisions surface and more opportunities present themselves. Other ideas come into play that supplement your current activities, and with a little effort your project expands. You develop ancillary businesses or investments that enhance the initial idea and add stability behind the momentum, and more ideas occur. You develop systems to handle what you have and those systems create options and markets previously unseen. Inertia – an interesting concept, but you must first ACT.

Look beyond the things you start. Early in the process, look at ancillary activities. If you are starting a small business, determine what businesses complement your product or service. What product or service do your target clients want or need that you can provide in a way that benefits them and your larger model? What relationships support your primary business focus and how can you get them on board? This is essentially an extension of the "Who do you know who" exercise, but it also plays into this concept very well. The more you develop places for the momentum to go, the faster and more effortlessly it will expand.

Develop infrastructure to manage stress, reduce friction and lighten the effects of gravity. A thousand years or so ago, a group of people who had escaped from the Aztecs created a series of cities and agriculture on small islands in the brackish waters off South America. The Aztecs allowed this culture to exist because of the extremely defendable position it enjoyed as well as the fact that the culture seemed to be literally isolated and had little hope for survival, let alone development. The people were a resourceful bunch having survived the ruthless Aztecs. A large number had even been Aztec slaves that escaped to their hideaway in a daring and well organized exodus. They had the materials on hand to build canoes, which they then filled with earth and planted crops in them; they drilled holes in the canoes and sank them in the water adjacent to their islands. They sank several canoes next to each other so they could create a platform onto which they built their homes, freeing up more land for crops. Their leader required each family to provide a canoe, and together they built a bridge to enhance their ability to get water; ironically, their scarcest resource. The leader then required every family to provide a certain amount of feet of Bamboo, which they engineered into a pipeline from their water source. These are my kind of people. They outlasted the Aztecs, if my memory serves.

Our office manager Dalaine develops systems and infrastructure for our clients and firm, and through her I have learned wonderful ways we can use technology to organize our information and ourselves. We did not have to hire consultants or purchase expensive and complex software programs to do what I wanted to do. She built, and continues to build, efficient pipelines using the tools we have on hand. These tools serve to reduce the daily pressures of tracking the financial lives of many people, and free us up to find ways to provide more and better services to our clients and time for our families. Thinking about the future and spending the time to create systems to track our activities allowed me to think about how we could provide our services in different ways at higher levels, with less time commitment. When we get lulls in activity I tend to focus on infrastructure. One time when I was apparently more urgent than normal about getting a project done, Dalaine made the comment that when I do not have a lot of clients flowing into my business I get uptight about infrastructure. The implication was that I should be focusing on business creation rather than infrastructure. My explanation ran along these lines: I have certain activities that I engage in that create business for the financial planning component of our firm. I teach 40 times a year or more, and try to do good work with those that are referred to me or come to us in one way or another. When the flow of clients slows it usually indicates to me that I reached or created some form of capacity issue as momentum developed in my business, but my inability to direct the momentum caused the flow to be reduced. Something about my business infrastructure or personal work habits created an impediment in my business. My job is to find and remove these obstacles as fast as possible so we can expand our business until we get to the next series of obstacles.

The Pastor at my church is a friend of mine and he told me about capacity and pushback in the growth of a church. Once a church gets to a place where 85 percent of the seats are filled for most services the church needs to expand, or create a mission church, or anticipate some decline in attending membership. The reason is that the congregation doesn't like feeling crowded and when new people come, they feel crowded, so the new people go somewhere else and the current members either go somewhere else or come less often. I think the same thing is true in any business endeavor; there are places where you either have to expand your capacity or the place will start feeling crowded and your momentum stalls. The good news for us is that we rarely have to build a larger sanctuary in order to get the job done, as the church probably needs to do if they intend to grow in numbers.

In theory, and usually in practice, we develop more momentum with each improvement. As your business and infrastructure expand, you can make quantum leaps in the quality and quantity of your results based on these incremental improvements. Remember that you only need to be a small, measurable amount better than average, and never quit, in order to be worth 10 times as much as the average in the marketplace. Often making one or two small changes can increase your effectiveness in one or more areas by 10 percent or more. If you concentrate on finding those opportunities, it is relatively easy to double your results.

Take the time to work on your business. If you could spend 20 percent of your time thinking deeply about how to expand your business, make it more efficient, or work on projects that directly impact the long-term success of your business or financial plans, what would the top 10 items of focus be? Brian Tracy, in his "Ultimate Goals" program, tells us to write out our 10 primary goals and to look at the list and ask, "If I could only do one thing, which one would it be?" Once you establish what the one item is that you would do above all others (usually the choice we make is the one that facilitates most of the other 10 goals), write down 10 things you can do to facilitate the best option available. Prioritize the list once you have it in place, and set about DOING the action items that are created by the activity. Once you have a primary task, ask yourself the question, "How can I implement X in my life in the most effective manner?"

Now write 20 legitimate answers to the question. Twenty is important because it causes you to stretch mentally. Some of the really good answers need to be mined from deep within your creative subconscious. Reaching those answers requires concentration, which the exercise of finding 20 answers develops in abundance.

I offer this as a way for you to develop enough mental fodder to make investing a large portion of your time in strategic development practical. I perceive that most people feel they cannot afford to take the time. Hopefully this process helps people understand they cannot afford not to. If you ask three questions per week for 50 weeks per year, you will develop 3,000 ideas intended to move you toward your goals. After a month you can look at your ideas and find where there are repeating ideas. These repeated items seem like good places to focus your attention. Dedicate a half hour every day to development. Three days asking questions, two days developing the ideas. Do this for a month and you may find another half hour to dedicate to the process. Perhaps you could ask, "How can I find another half hour to work on development without losing current momentum?" Remember that most people spend 20 percent of their time doing what makes money and 80 percent doing other things. Make a goal to use 20 percent of the time you are not spending actively engaged in making money to create ideas to expand your pipelines and increase your momentum. Robert Kiyosaki tells a great story about hauling buckets versus building pipelines. We have to find ways to stop hauling buckets. This is one great way, but clearly not the only way, to develop momentum. The opposite side of inertia is that an object, mind, or person at rest remains at rest until put into motion. Put your plans in motion and manage the momentum, then persist until you succeed.

Expand your business in a cooperative manner. The Ancillary Business Services chapter covers a great deal of this using a different context, but the essential idea is that you create business and marketing models that are highly synergistic with your primary business model. This has a tendency to keep things flowing in one direction and creates an environment where one solution affects many aspects of your business or financial life. People who are scattered all over in their activities have a hard time developing momentum in any area. If they do, they are easily derailed by some other non-essential, oft-unproductive task or crisis. Think about momentum as you develop your models; make it work *for* you rather than against you.

The pool analogy. When you play a game of pool, you first rack the balls (determine your best options and get them on the table) then you break rack, scattering the balls all over the table. From there, you have a series of options, some of which appear to be better than others. Your skill at implementing the next shot will determine how difficult or easy each ensuing step is. Like life, sometimes each shot you take gives you unexpected options, sometimes better than your original intentions, sometimes not. Usually, if you are working your plan, the easier shots get off the table early and the process of knocking them down keeps the game moving forward. Every so often we re-rack what's left and break again.

I know this analogy brings with it getting behind the eight ball. We have to watch for the compounding risks our shots may create, and not over-extend our ability to take another shot. One of the great ways the pool analogy expands is that in life, more balls are added to the table with every shot you take, making getting behind the eight ball less probable.

If you are, or would like to become, a small (or larger) business person, there are ways to best leverage your skills and relationships to enhance that opportunity. The following are some ideas to get you thinking. They are focused on one or two business models, but you should note opportunities where you could create similar results, wherever your interests lie. Remember that in this context, creating a small portfolio of real estate could look like a small business where you create a finite amount of relationships that you can use and leverage again and again.

ANCILLARY BUSINESS ACTIVITIES

I am generally motivated when working with the self-employed and small business owners to find ways to create business models that are synergistic with their current and primary business. There are a number of reasons for this and hopefully this narrative will spell out a few of them and develop a thread of thinking that you can apply in your ventures. It's important to note that these business models may in fact be marketing models for your primary business that have the look and feel of a business to them. When developed fully they often will produce their own profit centers, and sometimes they will simply be a way to profitably create business within your primary occupation. Since I work in the financial services industry and teach and otherwise support Realtors and real estate investors, my discussions are primarily focused on those who are involved in those fields. But we apply the same concepts to people in any line of work or business. The best reference I can think to give you is the book "Acres of Diamonds" which illustrates the fact that all the things we need for success are all around us; in the relationships we have, our unique skills and abilities, and the people and resources we choose to bring together. Another comment I would make about the idea that we are creating business models versus marketing models is that one implies a profit, the other an investment or expense. I hear salespeople talk about how they need to spend 10 percent or more on marketing, and I cringe. Not because marketing is not a good investment for many firms. It's because it brings with it the pressure to create "sales" to cover the expenses. It is my belief that we need to avoid being in transaction-related business models. It has also been my observation that heavy expenditures in marketing require a shortened sales cycle, and I cannot see how this can benefit the client in the long run. I propose that many of us can create ways to expand our business while investing time and energy into projects that will be lasting and at least pay for themselves, if not make a profit on their own. Another big advantage is that working in this way can help someone make the mental shift from self-employment into business ownership. If I ask a group of 50 Realtors how many of them are in business, 80 percent will raise their hands. When I ask how many could sell the business tomorrow, only one or two hands are left. This is not designed to be a slap in the face, or even to say that being self-employed is bad, but if we want our self-employment models to become business models we need to develop them that way. Let me give you an example of how a Realtor could do this.

A Realtor or anyone in sales has a name list, a contact list of acquaintances, friends, professionals, clients and so on. Some have developed these into databases that they communicate with on a periodic basis. They also have a natural service to deliver to their client, that their client needs and that the Realtor can help provide. Every homeowner, or even every adult, has certain needs as it relates to real estate or living in a certain geographical area. They need gutters and sprinkler system installers and repairers, they need landscapers and sheetrock guys, plumbers and roofers and the occasional furnace repair. They require legal and financial services, accounting and tax preparation. This list continues on and on of course. The Realtor can go to their list to see who they know who can provide those services, and for those they do not have they can seek referrals from their larger list to fulfill the need. In fact, asking for those referrals would be a good way to communicate the upcoming service enhancements your practice is implementing. You would then go to that list of service providers and become comfortable that their prices are competitive and that they would provide good service to your clients and good communication with you. You could also very reasonably ask for a referral fee from these service providers and I would suspect that most would have no problem with that. You will provide them with ready clients and they will have no outside costs to generate the business. If you ask for 5 or 10 percent, that would seem fair. There are certain businesses that cannot compensate you unless you have a series of licenses and/or credentials; the financial services, mortgage, insurance, real estate and legal professions are some that come to mind. If you're a Realtor, you should see if your broker would have a problem with this. The ones I have spoken with have applauded the effort. You would need to create agreements with the vendors and disclosures for your clients and/or your web site, as well as tracking systems to know who has been referred to whom. Many large firms already have concierge services in place, and integrating those into your practice would be effective; but in my estimation, less effective than creating your own. The Realtor would then need to invest in getting the new services onto their website and begin aggressively communicating to their database, and potentially their target audience, that their services exist. It may go without saying, but your clients would love a place where they could go to find what is needed in their area with the comfort that at least someone they know has a relationship with the plumber, or whomever. Your relationship with the vendor implies that they will do good work. The vendor sees you as a valued collaborative business partner and will go out of his or her way to make sure your clients are well taken care of.

You could ask your collaborative business partners to give you helpful articles that would add value to your clients, and to offer special values to them from time to time. this would create more contacts with your clients. The landscapers can hold seminars in conjunction with the nursery (which you also have a relationship with), which you would sponsor at no cost to you. A real-estate-minded financial planner could give seminars on property ownership and certain tax reduction methods that will help your clients. In some cases, they can help you sell real estate as well. You can drive more traffic to your web site, which in turn gives you the opportunity to showcase your practice more often. All of this will create new and future volume. I have no idea what the potential of the referral fees are because it depends on too many variables, but one would think it would more than pay for the web site and associated expenses. Your investment will be in time; meeting with the vendors, setting up the program and maintaining the ongoing communication. At some point the program will run smoothly and you can move on to the *next* way to benefit your now rapidly-expanding database *while* you are supporting your larger business.

Creating this stream of income and new business may allow you to add staff to support the effort. From there you can begin to add infrastructure to track the database more effectively and mine it more creatively. There are under-served niches in every industry; places you could make a few bucks if you only had the time. Your staff becomes your time. The idea being that over time you will create a series of residual lead and income sources, each of which has a business component and a longevity all of its own.

Now that you have converted a name list to a database with multiple places and reasons that your clients connect with you, you have more "evidence" that your *business* exists. The more ways you have to serve your clients the more valuable your business becomes to someone other than yourself, And, the more people there will be who would have an interest in acquiring it. Now you have a business you can sell, rather than a self-employment gig that ends when you do.

The creation of a business model that is more saleable to the outside world is one of the benefits of creating ancillary businesses. One of the unique, circular effects of this is that generally you will need to create team members to help run aspects of your business; associates to help facilitate your expanding primary business, and quality staff to help you create and maintain your infrastructure. In doing this you have created two more things. First, a group of logical purchasers of your business. It is likely the business would have more value and bring a better price if it were purchased by someone already familiar with your business and its potential. And the fact they know your customers, and your customers know them, is a real plus. If your key people would choose not to buy the business, you can sell your team and their expertise with your business.

This enhances its value substantially from a business without this type of infrastructure.

Second, the revenue created by the ancillary services will support your business financially. It will also allow you to track and enhance the number of times a client comes in contact with you in one way or another in the course of the year. This solidifies your position with your clients in creating potential future business, and confirms their value to your business. All of this works together to create a brand for your business, increased financial stability, increased traffic to your primary business, and increased loyalty and sales from your existing contact base -- all in the form of a profitable marketing plan.

This is another example of how you can use one or two investments, or in these cases, actions, to receive multiple rewards. I have spoken often about the need to triangulate investments; to make sure we receive multiple benefits and opportunities whenever we make an investment of time or dollars for financial gain. The more you do this, the more you will see other opportunities to apply this principle. Eventually, it becomes second nature. There are many people whom I come in contact with that do not want the headache of building a large business. These folks can simply apply this logic on a smaller scale.

I challenge you to write down a few of questions for yourself and then give yourself 20 legitimate answers to those questions.

First:
What services are in some way related to the product or service I deliver, that my current contacts or clients may use from time to time?

Second:
Who do I know who delivers services of any type in the community where my clients live?

Third:

> How can I build an inexpensive method to connect these services?

Fourth:

> What are 20 services related to my industry that my clients may use, and that I do not currently provide? (Follow up question: Can I provide the best of these services with little or no investment?)

Going through this process will lead you to other questions about how to implement the program. If you continue to legitimately ask and answer the questions and ask others for advice on points you feel you need help with, an action plan will quickly take shape as to how to best accomplish the tasks. Here are a couple of other examples to expand your context and hopefully make it easier to apply to your world.

I know a real estate investor who, in his first year of acquiring properties, accumulated 20 houses. His primary cash flow was developed in the acquisition of the properties themselves. He has a small cash flow from the properties to help offset vacancies and expenses. In analyzing his situation, we determined we needed to restructure his debt to increase his cash flow from the properties. This was unfortunate because he had just acquired the debt, but we find poorly structured debt more often than not. It also did not take long to determine that his growth had at least one limiting factor. Time invested in managing the properties was taking away from the time needed to focus on locating and acquiring new properties, as well as on the intelligent acquisition of debt -- the two things he ultimately will get paid the most to do. Because he has extensive relationships within the real estate investment community, as well as an excellent flair for developing new relationships, the most natural thing in the world for him to do is to create a property management company. In his market there is an opportunity to create a reasonably priced management service for single family and small multi-family properties. He has a good start when taking his properties into consideration. This service can be augmented by referrals to providers of services to his landlord clients as well as his tenants. In his case there is a synergy in the sense that he will invest his time and the required capital in creating a management company. It may temporarily conflict with his property acquisition business (although positive activity often produces unexpected positive results, so I would not be surprised if his business does not suffer) but in a year or so the property management firm may reach a tipping point where the revenues generated will compensate the staff required to manage the property effectively. If thoughtful marketing/business models were developed to deliver a flow of prospects into both sides of the business, the client would have a consistent and ever-expanding flow of referral income as well as increased profitability from both the property management and acquisition activities. As one benefit feeds another, the real estate investor has a consistent revenue stream to help support his desire to continue to acquire favorable debt, unaffected by the discount a lending institution makes to the value of the asset as a rental, or its income. There are in this case, dozens of services that will be needed once again, from Accounting to Windows and everything in between His firm could be both the direct and indirect provider of some of these services, but there is no reason to stop there. It would make sense for this entrepreneur to create a contracting firm that did certain remodeling and expansion projects for his clients and others. This works well in that it allows him to provide profitable yet reasonably priced services to his tenants, which in turn leads to increased business. The remodeling and repair business will also service other property owners, some of which may own and manage their own rental property. This leads to the opportunity to talk about property management and the price differential for services. As the client moves on he will likely create a retail real estate firm and enter into agreements to legally and ethically share in mortgage compensation, until it becomes necessary to acquire a mortgage company all his own. The cycle will continue as the real estate company helps people buy property that needs to be managed, repaired and maintained, and the tenants become homeowners. My recommendation would be to dedicate a couple of years to creating these pipelines and then check out the new landscape. The view will be quite different by then, and a new set of priorities and options will be well on their way to developing. The client would now have multiple businesses with multiple sources of income, one supporting another.

There is another case of a business in my town that has been there for a long time doing brake jobs and simple auto repair. It is run by a great bunch of dedicated people and they provide good service at reasonable prices. The size of our town and its attractiveness to businesses and investors has increased substantially over the past several years, and two new competing firms came to town with bigger and more visible stores. I know this has affected this man's business, yet up till now I have seen no change in his approach. How can he expand his offerings to his current loyal clientele, myself among them? This is the question he needs to write down 20 answers to. He could offer detailing. He is two blocks from two car washes and he has bays to do the finishing work. There is a section of his community that can afford a higher level of service; he should seek to provide it by any means available. He could become a manufacturer's rep for auto accessories and sell after-market products to his clients (He knows what they drive, for Pete's sake!). He could sell and install car alarms, stereo systems and auto starters. Their store is located next to a store that sells auto parts for do-it-yourselfers. Maybe they should teach classes to the customers of the auto parts store with the desire to generate clients when those same folks choose not to do certain repairs. There is no retail in the store, yet there is room for two racks... sell something! The people who come to your establishment are your assets. Give us something to buy; we are willing to support you. There are a dozen other things this business owner could do, but it will be up to the business to create a list of options and begin to implement them.

One more quick example: I was having a conversation with a financial services associate of mine and he was telling me about a simple discussion he has with his clients. He asks his clients about their auto insurance and finds that very often they have relatively low deductibles and relatively low limits of liability. In his example he spoke of people who carried a $500 deductible with liability of $100,000 per person or $300,000 per occurrence. I talked to a couple of property and casualty insurance agents and they told me this was fairly typical. My planner friend explained that most people would rarely file a claim for less than $1,000 and would almost never file two smallish claims within a 2-year period for fear their premiums would go through the roof. Yet what happens if you cause a significant accident and someone dies or becomes disabled? Someone sues you. Your insurance company covers the first $100,000 and the rest is up to you. "I find people insure their checkbook and leave their assets unprotected. I tell them to call their agent and increase their deductible and their liability protection. The net result costs about the same." He gives this thoughtful advice because he does not want a lifetime of work thrown away because his client did not understand the purpose of his auto insurance. He sought no reward or compensation. In fact to him it is, to some degree, an off-handed effort he does on the client's behalf. My friend ought to create a property and casualty company to supplement the services within his financial planning practice. It could be constructed much like the previous examples. Again, the question becomes "How can I inexpensively fill a need for my clients and prospects in a way that supports my larger business model?"

If you are someone who is considering starting a small business it seems reasonable that you would consider the various ways you can leverage yourself and your client base -- both as a way to consider the type of business to create, as well as how to develop a stable and profitable business through the use of the broader technique.

Who Do You Know Who?

When small business owners or self employed individuals seek to diversify their current offerings, expand their business model, create ancillary business services or exploit a market niche, one of the tools they can use for their benefit is a "Who Do You Know Who" primer.

If you're looking to expand your services as part of your marketing model or as a business venture, or you're looking to communicate a value-added sales-generating idea to a targeted group of people, this exercise will give you a place to start. I will attempt to create the primer around various activities that are currently supported or promoted by my own businesses, and you can expand on this to fit your circumstances.

Ask yourself this question and adapt the answer to the desired activity: "Who do I know who does, provides, or is, the following?" Get a pad of paper and write names by the questions. Ask your spouse and kids to help.

> ▶ A large, downloadable version of the following chart, and many other helpful tools, are available on the website: **www.creativewealthstrategies.com.**

WHO DO I KNOW WHO:

Activity	Does This		Provides This		Is This	
Sprinkler Systems						
Landscaping						
Driveways						
Snow Removal						
Lawn Care						
Roofing						
Siding Windows						
Doors						
Plumbing						
Window Treatments						
Painting (Normal and "Fancy")						
Cleaning Services						
Heating, Ventilating and Air Conditioning						
Drywall						
Masonry						
Trim Work						
Framers						

WHO DO I KNOW WHO:

Activity	Does This	Provides This	Is This
Stager			
Interior Designer			
Architect			
Gutters			
Handyman			
Moving Company			
Auto Repair			
Detailing			
Commercial Construction			
Sewing Machine Repair			
Vacuum Repair			
Car Dealerships			
Accountants			
Attorneys			
Financial Advisors			
Realtors			
Mortgage Companies			

Activity	Does This	Provides This	Is This
Furniture Companies			
Moving Companies			
Hair Salons			
Local Restaurants			
Nurseries			
Gardeners			
Teacher of Guitar Music Lessons			
Daycare Providers			
Limousine Services			
Catering			
Chiropractors			
Church Directory			
Self Employed People			
Business Owners			
Income Property Owners			
People Who Own Vacation Property			
Doctors			

WHO DO I KNOW WHO:

Activity	Does This	Provides This	Is This
Dentists			
Surgeons			
Accountants			
Corporate: Executives			
Human Resources Director			
Controller			
Runs a Not-For Profit			
Leader of a Church			
High Net Worth People			
People Who Earn In Excess Of $250,000 Per Year			
People Who Attend Self Help Seminars			
Who Owns a Home Valued at $400,000 oOr More			

These ideas support acquiring and rehabbing property, creating ancillary business services, creating a marketing niche, creating a sales niche, and identifying a quality target audience for some of the supporting services. If you were to make this into a complete marketing list you would also need some other headings like clients, prospects, parents of kids' friends, etc.

Now that you have established who you know and what your skills and passions are, and you understand the ability to interconnect those attributes, you are well on your way to creating an effective planning constitution. All you need to do now is write down all of the relevant facts and begin asking the right questions… How can I…?

Intelligent Debt Acquisition

I have mentioned the importance of intelligent debt acquisition multiple times and thought it would be good to explain some of what I mean.

The cost, or rate, of your note (mortgage, loan, etc.) is generally not as relevant as your ability to repay the note and get another one, so I am not advocating "cheap rates." I am not talking about buying your first home as much as looking to create a real estate portfolio. Real estate is just about the only asset where you can create effective debt, unless you are in a substantial company that can take advantage of factoring. Most rental properties will not cash flow well with less than 20% equity in them. As such, that is where the most favorable lending terms are. There are essentially two reasons to buy real estate: long term rental investments or property that you are going to improve (I am excluding buying and holding land in this discussion) and then sell. If all you do is buy, fix up and sell, then what you have created is a "job" -- you should always be looking to keep property. If you are doing this, you can affect a simple debt construction strategy that will reduce the dollars invested in the project.

Let's pretend we found a property that was selling for $200,000 but you determine that if you invest $50,000 in upgrades the house will be worth $335,000. Your $250,000 investment is 75% of the improved value. If you choose to keep the property as a rental it should cash flow due to the equity (all kinds of variables to consider, of course. I am just working on the debt construction.)

If you went to a bank you should be able to do this project with $50,000 down (20% of the $250,000 cost). If you have $50,000 you could put it in the bank and ask the bank to collateralize the $50,000, leaving it in an interest bearing account at their bank. If you did this, you could ask the bank to loan you the entire $250,000 for the project, based on the after-upgraded appraisal. You will need plans to get the appraisal done.

If you decided to keep the property you could get a "normal" loan for the $250,000 invested, plus closing costs, and still be below the 80% threshold. You should cash flow, have a couple hundred thousand in depreciating assets from an income tax perspective, and you have $335,000 in asset value which is growing. How much would you have invested? Zero. Since I think everything costs money, I made up the rule that everything that costs nothing costs $3,000.

Now, when we look at returns, let's pretend the house increases in value at 5%, you earn a whopping $1,000 per year in positive cash flow, and you receive a $7,000 per year tax deduction. If our investment were $3,000 we would be earning:

$1,000 income	33.33%
$7,000 deductions x 30% tax rate = $2,100	70%
$335,000 x 5% = $16,750 appreciation	558%

The appreciation improves every year as a percentage of the initial investment. The income tax deduction is static and the income is variable, but probably increasing. I can do all the Modern Portfolio Theory I want and never touch that return. Although this is a potentially extreme example, a well-constructed real estate portfolio will almost always out-perform equities (provided you own the property yourself as opposed to in a Real Estate Investment Trust, or REIT).

What if you don't have 50 grand or do not want to tie it up in this way? You can collateralize the equity positions of existing properties. For simplicity, let's say you have a $400,000 home with $250,000 in debt. Eighty percent of $400,000 is $320,000 -- the amount between the $250,000 you owe and the 80% can be collateralized. In this case, the bank can "hook" the equity by collateralizing it, and you can borrow the entire project cost that way. When you either sell the property or create permanent financing, the hook is released. You can then re-hook the property for the next project. Strategic debt reduction on rental properties will create more or better equity positions to leverage. Certainly not all banks will do these development-type commercial loans, but some will.

Another quick debt comment is that once you have developed a portfolio of properties, cluster them and affect strategic debt reduction. Identify properties that debt reduction will most positively affect from an income, loan provisions, or loan-to-value perspective. Properties that have in excess of 25% or 30% equity and 125% income-to-debt-service essentially become invisible -- or positive -- from a mortgage company perspective, whereas everything other than that is a negative. Creating one or two debts is relatively easy; it is getting to the 15th one that is hard. Doing them right from the beginning will allow you to have less of your own money invested, and will increase the ease and reduce the cost of the ensuing loans.

There are many resources for investing in real estate so I will not reinvent the wheel here. The point I want to make is that you should have a goal for either the number of properties or overall real estate portfolio value and get there as quickly as is safely possible. Time and tenants are the keys to success in a real estate portfolio (i.e., Don't wait to buy real estate, buy real estate and wait). And once you have *these* assets, you *really* have options.

The balance of this book involves taking what you have and improving on it, focusing on tax reduction, and addressing Will creation.

Once you own a business you have multiple options for tax reduction based on the dollars you are already spending, and the prudent trustee would make the most of them. The next two chapters deal with two fundamental forms of offensive tax reduction.

OFFENSIVE TAX REDUCTION

My Biological Mother Bobbye convinced me some years ago that I needed to get out of the restaurant business because she felt I had come as far as I could without getting back into restaurant ownership, which I did not want to do. She was right. She invited me to become a presenter promoting seminars put on by the Tax Reduction Institute (TRI) and Mr. Sandy Botkin (She now owns the company that markets the seminars). She did not intend for me to make a vocation of this, but she thought it would get me around some interesting people doing interesting things. She was right about that, as well. I was not a particularly good salesperson for TRI, but I was a fairly good speaker and took what opportunities I could to learn from my audiences and other presenters. I was at an event for the insurance industry when I watched a man do a presentation on Charitable Remainder Trusts. I was blown away by two things: First, I understood that he was telling me I could take assets that I already own and may want to liquidate and make them tax efficient. Second, out of a room of 70 people, there were only two of us actively engaged in what was being taught. Very few of these financial professionals got it, or cared. It was like someone went inside my head and turned on all of the lights. I learned that day that there was such a thing as defensive tax reduction, and what I was teaching (via TRI and Mr. Botkin) was offensive tax reduction. I also learned that there was a market for a person who could do both well, and my life has forever changed. After a considerable amount of education and experience in financial services since that day, I have recently come to break offensive tax reduction down into two broad categories. **Offensive tax reduction is the act of taking the dollars you are already spending and making them tax deductible -- morally, legally and ethically.** You must be in business or be self employed to use this effectively.

Offensive tax reduction is also the act, or art, of taking the assets you are using or building to generate income in retirement and managing their ownership, access and distribution to substantially reduce your current and eventual income taxes. In sum, I want to use this incentive-based tax system to my advantage (another reason NO ONE wants a flat tax.) We will focus on these two different concepts with the same name separately, starting with offensive tax reduction for income, retirement and estate planning.

This latter type of offensive tax reduction listed above is more subtle and impacting than the effort of deducting as many expenses as possible. It can take years to develop and can deliver a lifetime of benefits. It leads to a more dynamic discussion because every person's situation dictates the course that will work best for him or her. On the whole the concept is simple: Find ways to take the assets that you already own, or that you are developing, and make them income-tax-efficient in retirement -- and, if at all possible, before retirement. I find that most retirees did not develop their assets during their working lives with a strong consideration of how they would access the income from their assets in retirement. Interestingly, even while in retirement most people are not thinking enough about the tax output of their income.

In retirement we are going to receive income in the form of social security payments, pension distributions for those who have them, IRA distributions, rents for those who have rentals, and interest and dividend income from our investments. Some people also have royalties, stock options or the intent to sell assets. Few people have all of these assets at play or income choices this varied, but everyone falls in there somewhere. The percentage of social security that is taxed is determined by our annual taxable income. The amount of effective income tax we pay is determined by how far we go up in the tax brackets, as is our loss of personal exemptions. It would appear that taxes would be one of the things you want to control. I speak often about controlling those few things you can and working hard with the rest; this is a critical place to exert control.

If you own investment real estate in retirement, consider refinancing the property one year, taking out $70,000 and not withdrawing from the IRA for two years unless you are over 70 and forced to. The $70,000 would be tax-free and you would avoid paying tax on the social security. In fact, your taxable income would be your $10,000 pension, part of which would be sheltered (if you itemize) by the interest on the real estate loan. If you have enough income producing real estate you could do this indefinitely when interest rates are favorable. If not, consider doing something like this every third year. Once every three years you pay all those taxes, and the other two years you save $10,000 and defer $25,000. Of course you still have the $100,000 you did not withdraw from the IRA. Even if a person had no assets except their home and an IRA, this could be effective. You just need to look at your circumstances. The tax savings may more than accommodate taking on the debt.

If a person does not have real estate there are other actions they could take. Simply taking distributions from an IRA every other year would help in the context of social security. If a person has an individual equities portfolio, they can sell high basis stock from time to time and use those resources as income. People tend not to want to touch the principal in these accounts, ignoring the tax potential being lost in holding them. They can always buy them back, using the IRS's money. I do not know today which choice I would recommend in the future. What I do know today is that the more options I have the better, and with them we can match a strategy to whatever tax, income, or market realities we are facing at the time. This is a critical aspect of creating an effective income plan: creating assets with different tax characteristics and opportunities so you can create the best possible tax consequence in accessing your income. When you pay less in taxes, your balance sheet grows faster and the more opportunities you have to create diverse assets.

Creating real estate portfolios creates offensive tax reduction on both fronts. You can create a steady stream of tax deductions, in some cases using them to reduce taxes on "other" income in the early years of building the portfolio, in addition to the ability to access the equity of your property in a number of different ways, including:

- Refinancing when interest rates allow

- Selling when prices and/or taxes are favorable

- Selling on CD when interest rates are high, or

- Exchanging into a like-kind property to enhance cash flow.

All of these tax-favored opportunities involving real estate are available because our tax code and economic policy strongly support property ownership and understand its value to the community and the country as a whole. If you are someone who understands the value of owning real estate but cannot stand the idea of being a landlord, consider hiring a property manager. It will have an affect on your cash flow but you are usually in it for the growth and eventual access to income and equity anyway.

For people who still cannot stand the idea of using income producing real estate as an asset I have another idea that may allow you to manage your taxes and/or your income in retirement -- life insurance. Yeah, I thought that would wake you. I refer to insurance as a solution at different places for different reasons throughout this larger text, and this is another place where it has unique benefits if understood and used properly.

Insurance and its proper use is an enormous topic and could take hundreds of pages to describe thoroughly. Where a few others and myself would find that interesting, no one else would, so I will tighten it up considerably. The reason that insurance is considered a lousy investment is because usually it is. When you are growing a family and a business you often purchase term insurance, which offers an excellent return on investment provided you die. That's a long way to go to get a result. Otherwise the policy, like over 90% of term insurance polices, lapses with no benefit paid or cash value.

Cash value insurance purchased for estate tax protection is generally death-benefit driven. When constructed properly, these polices are not cash rich. There is no advantage in funding them in a way to make them effective from an investment perspective. Unless the policy is performing multiple functions for the family (a whole other story) it is primarily death-benefit driven. These policies generally have a decent rate of return no matter when you die, unlike the term where you need to be in a hurry, but generally do not provide any income benefit (although it can be used in wealth creation as explained in other discussions). Occasionally someone who is older than 50 will have a need for insurance for 20 years or more, but not necessarily until death. Sometimes in those cases you should consider a universal life (UL) policy (probably not variable unless you are very bullish) instead of a 20-year or longer term. You need a quality insurance agent to check multiple carriers to look at the outcomes. Often, even though you pay more annual premium for the UL, the projected cash values may give you all of your money back in 20 years, where the term will be worthless. Be careful and choose your advisor wisely. This is a big investment and we see more incorrectly designed polices than we do correctly designed ones. For many people term is still the better answer.

Now we can get to how to fund these for retirement income. The key to making an insurance policy work from an investment perspective is to buy the least amount of death benefit possible while funding the policy at the highest legal limit. The tax code has limits to the amount of money you can put into an insurance policy and still have the policy maintain its unique insurance characteristics. (The IRS understands that these can be good investments). If you invest too much in the policy it becomes a modified endowment contract, or MEC. When that happens you are taxed like an annuity. When you withdraw money it is interest first, fully taxable. If we stay under these MEC limits we get insurance taxation -- return of investment first, interest second. Insurance also has the unique characteristic of allowing for loans, which are of course free of tax. Many people withdraw the principal and borrow the interest, avoiding tax on all of the income they use from the policy.

The advantage of buying a low death benefit is that the cost of insurance is one of the big things weighing down the investment effectiveness of the policy. As you put cash in your contract, the insurance benefit, when constructed for these purposes, usually stays the same, at least for a while. The spread between the cash you have saved in your contract and the amount of the death benefit is the net amount at risk to the insurance company. The closer you can get those numbers to each other the more effective your policy will be, because there will be less at risk to the insurance company and lower expenses to you. These policies also become very effective self-funded bank accounts where you can efficiently access cash for other "outside" investments, like real estate. In fact, many serious real estate investors ought to have an effective insurance component to their planning. Unfortunately we often find people who bought a policy for "investment" purposes and are funding it at minimal levels. These policies are black holes. They may eventually be a cost effective way of providing death benefit (if the stars line up) but they will never be effective investments. When done properly, however, over-funding a life insurance policy can create a tax-free pool of cash for you to access in retirement to offset withdrawals from more taxable investments. As mentioned in another discussion many people have confidence in accessing the equity position of their home later in life because the insurance death benefit will be there for their heirs. This gives you another option to explore. If you bought the exact same investments outside the insurance policy, the rate of return will of course be higher, because insurance polices are generally expensive places to do business. The **result** of using an insurance policy in conjunction with other effective income planning will be greater than the non-insurance option, even though it is more expensive. It is not the price, but the cost -- or result -- that matters.

I referred earlier to this type of offensive tax reduction as the *art* of taking the assets you are using or building to generate income in retirement and managing their ownership, access and distribution to substantially reduce your current and eventual income taxes. It is an art because every plan is unique and needs to fit your personality and your circumstances. It is why we have appointment after appointment with our clients helping them and us establish what works for them, with their assets, their skills, the opportunities and obstacles created by their relationships, and the type of larger plan they seek to create. Only then will we know all of the tools we have to work with in order to build a lasting and significant plan for the future. I was just thinking that this is an arts and crafts business. You need to be an artist as well as a craftsman. You have to be able to not only see it, but build it as well.

STRATEGIES

FOR SELF EMPLOYED OR SMALL BUSINESS OWNERS

Offensive Tax Reduction is the act of taking the dollars you are already spending and making them tax deductible -- morally, legally and ethically.

In an effort to control all that we can control about our financial future, we need to employ every legal device reasonable to reduce taxes on our earned income. We are talking about tax avoidance, not tax evasion. There are a number of differences -- the largest being about 2 to 5 years (the time you'd spend in jail, that is).

The people who can best take advantage of offensive tax reduction strategies are self-employed people, small business owners or people who own enough real estate to be considered professional real estate investors.

the things I try to do is to help people think of taxes as
Another is to have them think of taxes as a negotiable
_ all have to pay a certain amount of taxes based on the
income we earn. To the extent we can reduce our tax burden we
are increasing our income, or "renegotiating our bill." If I asked
you to spend 5 minutes a day to increase your income by $5,000
per year, you would jump at the chance. Unless, of course, you're
earning in excess of $300 per hour consistently, in which case
you can afford to pay someone to spend the 5 minutes a day
it would take to earn it. If I told you that if you spent 20 hours
writing letters, supplying information and waiting on hold with
the bank you could reduce your mortgage by $400 per month
indefinitely, you would find the time to do that, too. Many self-
employed people can create the $10,000 to $15,000 in new
deductions required to create that $5,000 per year result, and
they don't have to spend an extra dime to do it!

I am not going to try to teach you many specific techniques in
this text. Understand that like most things, planning is highly
individualized and every business and individual can use
different techniques. I will also point out that I am not trying
to substitute as a CPA here. As you employ these techniques,
all of the deductions you take must be supported, as your
CPA will tell you. It is dangerous to assume your accountant is
taking care of your taxes. It is also dangerous to rely on so-called
"gurus" like me. We will try to give you tools and techniques to
create simple, effective record keeping, but YOU are in charge
of following up. A great reference for you is a book called "How
to Save Money on your Taxes" by Sandy Botkin. Sandy is a CPA
and tax attorney and once worked for the chief council to
the IRS in Washington, DC. He teaches far more in that book
about practical application of these principles than I know, let
alone could include in the body of this work. He also has a live
presentation I strongly recommend. You can learn more about
it (or get his book for that matter) on my website or call 1-888-
376-8607. Sandy actually is a guru in this area, but the effort
and organization still belongs to you. My primary motivation
for discussing offensive tax reduction is to get you motivated

to work on it, to give you a few resources to check out, and to remind you that in tax reduction, as in many things, we are just a few small steps from having a dramatically different outcome than the one we currently have (either positive or negative).

Here are a couple of examples: We all use a vehicle in our business, yet most people severely under-utilize this important deduction. The IRS gives us two methods to deduct our automobile. First is the IRS method, where you determine your business miles driven and deduct the amount they allocate per mile (around 40 cents at this time). Second is the Actual method, where you actually track your expenses (i.e. gas, oil, etc.). I have done an unofficial survey of thousands of Realtors over the years by asking the question in seminars I teach. About 15 percent of the people use the Actual method, 70 percent use the IRS method, and 15 percent don't know what method they use, if any.

If there is a method referred to as the IRS method and a different method called anything other than the IRS method, which is generally better for you? Anything that is not the IRS method, of course. You didn't need me to tell you that. So why don't you use the Actual method? Too complicated? Let's take a look at two things: What you are giving up, and what complexity you are avoiding.

First, I was told that the actual average cost to drive a mid-size car was around 62 cents per mile, and the IRS was offering 40. If you averaged 62 cents per mile you would increase your deduction by 158%. In other words, if you currently drive 15,000 business miles, you deduct around $5,400. If you got 62 cents you would receive a deduction of $8,550. The additional $3,150 in deductions is worth between $1,000 and $1,500 to you in real cash. That is worth at least SOME complexity. Let's see how much. The Actual method consists of tracking your depreciation (which your accountant does, or you can use a depreciation table), your insurance (which you get reported to you annually), your interest, if you have any (which gets reported to you

ally), major auto repairs (in your glove box), and all the rest:
il, parking, car washes and wiper blades.

The only things you *really* have to track are the "rest" items. Sandy has what he calls the shoebox technique. Take a shoebox, cut a whole in the lid, tape the top down, and put it in your car. Whenever you get a receipt, put it in the box (or the compartment in your car) and at the end of the year, have a cup of coffee and add up all the receipts. Over the course of the year you may have spent a total of a half hour putting receipts in the box, another half hour gathering the insurance and bank information and putting them on a ledger, and an hour adding up the receipts. That 2-hour investment may create $1,000 or more. Is it worth it? It nets out to 20 seconds a day! It requires a small change in habit: Put receipt in box. There are a lot of other things that take a small amount of time and pay similar rewards.

Another excellent example of using the tax code to enhance your life as well as your wallet occurs when we have the opportunity to hire our children (or grandchildren). When we hire our children we are not subject to FICA or unemployment compensation or the rest of those taxes, and your children are entitled to a certain amount of income (as are all Americans) tax-free every year. Right now the number is around $4,500. If you hire a child or grandchild they should be at least 7 years old and need to not only be capable of, but actually doing, work for your enterprise. Depending on the business you're in, this could be easy or impossible at the age of 7, but there is precedent that says 7 is old enough to be employed if you can demonstrate that the child works in the event of an audit. When you hire children there are several things you have to do in order for it to be legitimate. Write an employment plan so everyone understands the job description. You need to complete the proper paperwork, a W-4 and an I-9 and an end-of-year W-2 (your accountant or the IRS website has this information.) You should pay regularly and by check. You should keep timecards, or have your child create and keep them as one of their responsibilities.

This strategy will take dollars that would be taxed to you and shift them to a place where they are tax-free. If you have no desire or ability to part with $4,500 by giving it to your child, here is a strategy I have seen used that delivers multiple benefits. You can set up a custodial checking account at the bank where you can sign checks, or you and your child can sign checks, but your child cannot independently sign checks. From this account you can pay the electric bill, the phone, cable, Internet or school lunch bill. You can buy clothes and pay for sports activities. Even groceries can come out of that account. Is it likely that you spend $4,500 per year on those types of things? Heck, most children probably cost that much in direct expenses if you add it all up, but to make it simple I would pay recurring expenses from that account. In my household we use auto withdraw to spend most of that monthly income and leave a bit for their smaller expenses, so they see some direct benefit for themselves.

One huge fringe benefit of setting this up is that the kids get a good sense of how fast money goes. Your children will learn what it costs to go grocery shopping when they write a check every now and then. Balancing their checkbook could be one of their tasks and they will learn from that, as well. If you want the money to accumulate for college you have funded it with pre-tax dollars, which is a good thing. If you use the pre-tax cash to buy property for the child, you will compound the tax benefits for their current and future benefit.

This leads us back to that other form of offensive tax reduction. Funny how that works.

STRATEGIES FOR BUSINESS OWNERS, EXECUTIVES AND PROFESSIONALS

Business owners should look to their own assets for business succession and estate planning. There are some long standing estate planning tools that would serve business owners well in creating a business succession plan. One of the great features of these tools is that they utilize assets that we already own and benefit from. There is a particular family of trusts known as Grantor Retained Income Trusts or GRITS that allow people to transfer an asset into a trust for the benefit of others, but retain the benefits of the asset for themselves for a period of time.

When you want these tools to be effective from a gift tax perspective, they need to take one of two forms. The asset transferred into the trust needs to be either a qualified personal residence, like your vacation home, or an asset subject to an annuity. Since the term "annuity" describes about a hundred arrangements, we should note that in this context annuity means a fixed income stream for a period of years.

Let's pretend that you own the building that houses your business, and you own it outside of the business, either personally or in a pass-through entity. You are collecting rent from your company(s). In this case, you could transfer the building into a trust referred to as a Grantor Retained Annuity Trust, or GRAT, and retain the income for a period of years. Let's pretend 15 years.

When you do this, three important things happen: First, the asset value freezes for gift tax purposes according to the tax code. Your building will not increase in value, according to the IRS. The second thing that happens is that the asset becomes creditor-proof. Because we have split the ownership into retained and remainder interests, it is virtually impossible for someone to sue you or your kids and gain access to the asset. Lastly, and most importantly from a gift tax perspective, the IRS has a formula that establishes the value of the retained and remainder interests. As of this writing the IRS says that all assets in a trust of this type earn around 4.5%. If you had a $1,000,000 building and paid yourself 9.5% or $95,000 per year. you would retain 5% more per year than you created. So for a 15-year trust you will have retained 75 percent of the trust's value (5 percent times 15 years). In our example, the asset began with a

$1,000,000 value. If you retained $750,000, then $250,000 is the value of the remainder. You make that gift using unified credit so it costs you nothing out-of-pocket. What will the value of the building be in 15 years? Who knows. For simplicity, let's say it doubled in value (around 5 percent growth). The gift tax result is that the $1,750,000 difference between the IRS-assumed remainder value and the actual value bypasses your estate for tax purposes, saving you something like $850,000.

What does this have to do with business succession? Simple. You are either going to transfer this business to your kids, sell it to some or all of your employees, or sell it to a third party. If you transfer it to your kids, the IRS is your partner and all efforts to reduce their position are warranted (and think of the insurance premiums you just saved). If you sell the asset to anyone else, you are going to have to manage the taxes on the transaction. Any rents paid to you by your company create an immediate tax deduction to the company, whoever owns it, which will help the buyer. You will undoubtedly want to sell the stock of the company to avoid double taxation. The buyer will want to buy assets to create tax deductions and avoid attendant liability. Most companies can "get around" the liability issue buy language and agreement, but the tax issue looms large in every transaction. To the extent we can create ordinary deductions for the buyer and not negatively affect the seller, we should do so. A blend of leases, stock and asset sales will often create the best result. This will allow the buyer to pay less and the seller to receive more, generally at the expensive of the "IRS partner." This is okay since the IRS is not all that invested anyway.

This concept also works with equipment. If you have depreciated equipment that your company uses, you may want to take advantage of the dividend distribution tax and distribute the assets to yourself at book value (your company will likely have some recapture). You will lease the equipment to the company, creating passive income for you and active deductions for your company. If you have a tax concern and these assets will hold up (there are clearly some assets that will work better in this environment than others), you may want to use a GRAT. You have simply created another method to take the assets that you already own and make them tax efficient.

How to utilize languishing assets

Do you have cash values inside of universal life insurance contracts languishing at 4% or 5%? Based on the long-term nature of the investments involved, do you see that situation improving markedly in the near to mid term? Would you like a multi-benefit opportunity to utilize that cash value for your increased benefit without giving up control of the policy or loss of its death benefits? To do this you could use a form of factoring accounts receivable we hear so much about these days. Cash value of life insurance, particularly when the policies are paying low interest, is the ultimate un-performing accounts receivable. I am not saying people should not have cash value life insurance. On the contrary, it is my opinion that owning such polices creates a great deal of flexibility for the policy's owner, and when taken advantage of, these opportunities can lead to fantastic overall wealth creation for the owners and/or their beneficiaries. Our challenge as financial advisors is in finding and taking advantage of the unique opportunities that best apply to the equally unique individuals that make up our financial services practices. The following is one example of how someone might take advantage of this strategy.

Let's assume that you have a policy that has a loan available of $250,000 and that currently is earning 5%. Let's also assume it would cost one half of one percent as a service charge to facilitate the loan. The effect would be that if you re-paid a loan to your contract at 6%, only 5-1/2% would be credited to your account.

I propose you consider borrowing the $250,000 from your account and investing it in 10 new single-family rental properties. You will need to analyze the policy to see how long the amortization schedule would need to be to help support the policy, but for this example I am going to assume 30 years. You will see in the example that this loan can be repaid much earlier than that if the situation warrants it. I will explain at the end of this narrative how the purchase of these properties could be done in a way that reduces your involvement in property management and increases your leverage.

Rather than create an extensive spreadsheet I decided to write a narrative, which you would need with the spreadsheet anyway. The "numbers" are straightforward enough and for the most part are guesses, except for the amortization numbers, which will be accurate based on the assumed interest rate. Here we go:

Assume that you invest $250,000 in 10 homes costing $150,000 each. You put 10% (or $15,000) down on each house for a total of $150,000. You hold the other $100,000 in escrow (presumably the majority of which would stay in your insurance contract for closing costs and window treatments, potential negative cash flows initially from the 100% financing arrangement [90% traditional, 10% insurance policy], as well as a hedge against monthly obligations arising from vacancies.) Assuming $1,000 miscellaneous acquisition expenses per house, you would hold $90,000 in escrow. This is around nine months of payments with all houses vacant. (We would not acquire these properties all at once and would get them rented as we went, so this is a virtual impossibility as an opening result.) The homes in this example are brand new and the cash flow is a paltry $1,000 per year, before you repay the lost interest on the loan from the policy. You will get the benefit of depreciation deductions, as well. Residential rental property is depreciated over 27.5 years. If we assume $125,000 per house as depreciable ($25,000 land) you will get a deduction of $4,500 each house for a total of $45,000 in tax deductions. This will only be useable against the passive income generated by the homes ($5,000 per year in the early years) plus you can use $3,000 in passive losses against ordinary income. In most situations there are strategies we might employ to accelerate the use of these deductions, but to the extent that we do not use them now they will accumulate for our future benefit. For example, if you sell your cabin in five years with a $200,000 gain, some portion of it (let's say $100,000) would be sheltered from taxes due to these deductions carried forward. The bottom line is, we will not lose them and we will have the opportunity to use them even if it is with the eventual sale of the real estate creating them.

You have now acquired $1,500,000 worth of real estate. In order to evaluate your investment we will need to make some assumptions:

Houses grow at 5% per year ($75,000 first year).

Income is $0.00 per year (for the first three years you "lose" a total of $30,000, then you should have positive cash flow, even after repaying the policy loan).

Tax effect is $16,000 ($45,000 times a 36% tax rate).

Investment is $250,000.

Returns are:

Growth, $75,000 on a $250,000 investment	30%
Initial cash flow $0,000 per year	0%
Tax effect $16,000 per year	6.4%

It is likely you will not use the entire $250,000 in creating this portfolio, which will of course increase your return on investment percentages exponentially.

Please project forward 14 years. Your homes are now worth $3,000,000 and your total debt is $1,015,000. You have benefited from $616,000 in tax deductions, worth over $200,000 to you. Your annual income has increased to at least $70,000 per year. You will have the flexibility to borrow from, liquidate or let these investments ride. Any choice you make will be tax favored (in relation to most other investments) based on the laws as we see them today (the capital gains rate is pretty much always lower than ordinary income rates and I can't see the deprecation deduction going anywhere, so we are not heavy on legislative risk in this proposal.) If we can favorably borrow money in the future, as we can now, we could easily "strip" $200,000 tax-free from this portfolio on an annual basis for the rest of your life. If you can live on that you would be set for life.

There is a risk of compression in the rental market, which could cause your limited cash flow to reverse at times. If you are buying at a time when rents are already depressed, only lower interest rates would drive them much further down. You have some near-term risk of lost equity if the housing market softens, which it may, due to increasing interest rates. This would make your property more rentable, however, and should ameliorate the lost equity problem unless you were forced to liquidate for some reason. I am supremely confident that over an extended period of time these homes will appreciate, and as long as we can keep them rented most of the time and own them for a while, the investment risk is minimal. There is a heightened level of B.S., to be sure, but you can do this in a way as to keep it as simple as possible for you.

I perceive the BS and risk to be well worth it. If we could find a safe, tax-deferred investment for your $250,000, paying 5%, you would have a whopping $500,000 accumulated, $250,000 of which will be taxable as ordinary income. That's more than $1,500,000 less than the investment I just discussed. I could be wrong by a fair bit and still have a great result. In addition, your life insurance policy is actually enhanced, because in this example you were paying 6.0% interest into your policy. If the insurance company kept .5 % for administration, your policy is being credited 5.5% -- .5% more than it is receiving currently; tax deductible to you, of course.

What say ye?

Now I am going to take you into the weeds a bit. Understand the above before entering these waters. The portfolio just described is an excellent investment and it has worked for people since

Babylonian times. We could get creative and smart about how we employ it in your unique circumstances.

You may have or need a Family Limited Partnership (FLP) with the need to fund or diversify it. You may also have a need to accumulate wealth to fund a buy-sell agreement, or for your retirement, or both.

You may want to create a separate Limited Liability Company (LLC) for the purpose of owning property rather than the FLP, but the idea is essentially the same. Assuming we can incorporate the details of how all of this might work, let's pretend we bought the houses in an entity owned by you and your kids, where you have the control but some or most of the ownership lies with the kids. Let's also assume we could apply a form of factoring to your accounts receivable in or out of your insurance policy. Consider the result: We took an unproductive asset, our accounts receivable, and used it to create wealth outside the company or policy to serve the interests of the companies, or polices owners. The $250,000 in question becomes creditor protected in the process. In the event of a buy-out internally, you would have this asset and its potential income to help facilitate it. In the event you sell the company, you could borrow equity from the LLC's assets and use it to purchase your insurance policies from the company (if your company or profit sharing plan owns them), if you wanted to. If your split dollar gets unwieldy, we could fund a roll-out using these tax-free dollars.

There are many other synergies involving your insurance policies and a real estate portfolio, whether you do this in conjunction with your long-term succession plans or as individuals.

There are many details one would need to work through to facilitate a plan using receivables, but the outcome could be quite simple, or quite complex, depending on how many benefits we try to squeeze from the strategy. Don't get too bogged down in the details of the enhancements I have added to the base plan. Understand the massive positive leverage involved and I am a happy guy.

Protecting your property using retained and remainder interests

Many professionals these days are interested in finding ways to protect their assets from predatory creditors. Doctors are leaving their home states, fields of specialty, or the field of medicine altogether because of the reality that either insurance premiums, or a well dressed lawyer, could take away all of the assets they worked a lifetime to accumulate. Many business owners stop delivering certain vital services due to fear of lawsuit by any number of special interest groups. But when you talk to your attorney about the problem the response usually goes something like: "If you want to truly protect your assets, you must give them away." This usually puts a damper on the conversation.

What if you could "give away" your assets in such a way that you would not really notice the effects for many years, if ever? What if you could do this in such away that you could save current income taxes as well as future estate taxes? What if you could do this and never lose control of your assets? What if it could be done using assets you already own and a plan that utilizes laws that have been well tested and on the books for years? Too good to be true?

Many of us already own the assets we can use to create asset protection plans. That's the problem; we OWN the assets. Whether the asset is held individually or jointly with a spouse, it is totally exposed to creditors, including the Internal Revenue Service. Property ownership is a critical issue in the way an asset protection plan might be constructed. We talked about individual and joint ownership. These are common forms of ownership that most people understand. There are other forms of property ownership that are less understood and less obvious. We will focus on the ownership of retained and remainder interests in this example.

If you owned an interest in an asset that lasted for some period of years (lets use 15), you would own a retained interest in that asset. Whoever owned the interest in the asset after the 15 years was used up, would own the remainder interest. The IRS has long-established formulas that help advisors and taxpayers calculate those values on an asset-by-asset basis. These are two very underutilized forms of ownership.

How does this fairly simple change in ownership create a situation where the underlying asset is unattractive and unavailable to creditors?

First, the Qualified Personal Residence Trust (QPRT) is an irrevocable trust that has two classes of beneficiaries and one or more trustees. The trustees have a fiduciary responsibility to both types of beneficiaries. It would be a breach of their fiduciary duty to jeopardize the interest of the remainder beneficiary in order to satisfy a debt (judgment) of the income beneficiary, or vice versa.

Let's look at how this might play out. You transfer your residence into a QPRT and retain the ownership rights for 15 years. After 15 years the beneficiary is either the trust itself for the benefit of your kids, a partnership that you control, or the children themselves. At the end of the 15 years you pay rent to the trust or the partnership, and that entity pays the taxes, insurance, gas, electric and the like. As long as the trustee (you) decides that this is a good arrangement the asset stays in trust (or partnership). If someone were to sue you, your ownership would be of a remainder interest of the use of the asset, and the trustee could not compel the remainder beneficiaries to give up any of their rights in the trust. This would cause an attorney to move to greener pastures.

You have not lost control of the asset and can enjoy it for as long as you like, if structured properly.

When you did this you not only protected the asset from creditors, you created a painless way to reduce your estate taxes. Both the retained ownership interest and the remainder interest have a value. It is the IRS tables' pegging of the value that makes this an effective tool for tax purposes.

When you set up a trust like this you are making a gift of the remainder interest to your children, and that gift is taxable. The IRS has tables that help us determine the value of the gift. To create an easy example, if a 60-year-old set up a trust for 15 years in today's interest environment, and transferred a $200,000 cabin to it, the IRS would perceive the present value of the gift made to the beneficiaries 15 years in the future to be around $88,000. Unless you have already used your $1,000,000 exemption, you will not have to pay a tax on the gift. If the cabin becomes worth $500,000 before the present owner dies, their estate will avoid approximately $200,000 worth of estate taxes. It is a repeal-proof plan if you intend to keep the property or one like it for the balance of your life. Why not pass it on with much less tax? If the government repeals the tax, you break even. If they keep it, or reinstate it, you win. Repeal-proof.

It can also be an effective way for a business owner to work on tax-effective equalization of the estate to include children in and out of the business. These trusts should be set up to work in concert with other strategies to maximize the value of your assets from a lifestyle, as well as business, financial and tax perspectives, and should generally serve to reduce your ultimate legal fees and insurance premiums.

None of this planning should be done in a vacuum. High-net-worth individuals and business owners need to seek out advisors who understand the myriad of choices offered by the tax code and have the vision to recognize where to apply them. It may be that there are tools more suited to you than this one, even if this tool seems perfect to you today.

WILLS & TRUSTS -
EXPLANATION OF TERMINOLOGY

Will and Trust documents will do far more than create mechanisms for the reduction of taxes. These documents will determine how your children/grandchildren will be raised and by whom, the amount of resources available to them for college, when they receive money once they become adults, as well as what happens if they pass away prematurely. It also stipulates who is to be the trustee of these resources and who will administer the estate upon your collective deaths.

DEFINITIONS OF THE TYPES OF INDIVIDUALS REQUIRED TO CREATE A WILL AND/OR TRUST:

PERSONAL REPRESENTATIVE:

Typically this person handles the administration of your final tax returns, and collects and distributes assets to your respective trusts and beneficiaries. This person's primary attributes should be organization and perseverance.

Typically, if you are married, you are each other's representatives at the first death. You are essentially naming a "successor" in the sense that this person's function will not come into being until the second death or in the event of a common disaster.

Often, as people get older, a child/grandchild emerges as the one who is most familiar with, and capable of assisting with, your day-to-day affairs. This person becomes a logical personal representative. Ultimately you are looking for the person best suited to step in and take care of organization, bill paying, and eventual reporting of these activities in the event of your death or severe disability. The sad truth is that far more of us will rely on this person during our lifetime than we think; one of the side effects of longer living.

Personal Representative Names	Phone Number	Comments

GUARDIAN:

Choosing this person or persons is, of course, the most important decision you will need to make in this planning process. You need to take into consideration whether or not the guardian(s) you choose can accommodate your children/grandchildren, or if you would need to help them in some way. For example, by making their home larger or allowing the use of your home while the kids are in school. It may be that none of this support is necessary, but it's better to determine this now so the trustee does not have to. You want to make it easy for the guardian to interact with the trustee, and that type of decision in the beginning of the relationship is pretty tough. Due to the obvious conflict of interest reasons, you usually do not want the trustee and the guardian to be the same person(s). People do not always take into consideration the difficult position the guardian is in as it relates to the assets of your children/grandchildren, particularly if they are the trustees as well. This is either because we just never think about it or because we do not think through the amounts of money we may be leaving our children or grandchildren.

Let's look at a scenario I have seen often in my practice. A young couple has two or three children, ranging from ages 2 to 12. Their net worth while living, including a couple of 401(k) plans and their home equity, is $200,000. They are struggling to find ways to expand their wealth either through business or investment opportunities. They each earn between $30,000 and $70,000 and have a $500,000 term policy on one, and a $200,000 policy on the other. Remember we are writing these wills in the event you die tomorrow, either or both of you, and the distributions you choose for the kids are based on your being dead. When you pass away your personal representative will pay all of your final medical bills, your funeral expenses and any outstanding near-term debt you may have. Most documents call for the payment of all debts, which could include your homes and other real estate that you may prefer stay mortgaged. (In that case you will want to strike or modify that *standard* sentence.) In our example, we have two kids ages 2 and 9. The trustee will pay to the guardian amounts necessary to provide for the children's health, education, maintenance and support (HEMS). Some portion of the food bill, the electric bill, all of the additional health insurance, life insurance on the kids if desired, clothes, school lunches and functions, sports and other special activities will all be accounted for and paid by the trustee to the guardian. How much can all that amount to? Let's say $10,000 per year. (Which seems pretty high to me, at least until the kids are driving?) Remember our clients have $200,000 plus $700,000 in death benefits. Let's say the final expenses were $100,000 (again, a pretty high figure). That leaves in trust $800,000 for the benefit of the 2 and 9 year old. The $10,000 per year expense would represent 1.25% of the trust amount. If the trust appreciated at just 6%, leaving 4.75% per year in growth, the trust will have grown to be worth $1,275,000 by the time the 9 year old turns 19. Assume we provide the oldest with $20,000 per year to go to school and increase our spending to $30,000 per year; the trust will grow to be worth something like $1,630,000. Now, how would it be if you are the guardian and you are working hard to provide for your now-extended family, and you were in control over this kind of money in trust? Can you feel the resentment mounting? It would be very difficult for the guardian to avoid determining that a boat -- or for that matter, a lake home -- ought to be considered part of HEMS. Having a stress-free life for the parents will be to the benefit of the child, so the vacation budget increases. Perhaps

: would create family disunity in the eyes of the guardian if ɑll of the kids (after all, these are brothers and sisters) do not have the same educational opportunities. Of course, while we all want to think that our friends or family would never do this, we have to understand human nature, especially when it comes to money. Why put the person in this unsustainable position in the first place? Just name two different people. This illustration also underscores the need for distribution ladders if you have young children or if you are leaving money to your kids with the grandkids as beneficiaries should your child(ren) die. Many wills distribute the trust upon the child reaching age 21 or 23. How would you like to dump half of a $1,650,000 trust on a person at age 21? Can you say Lamborghini?

Guardian Names	Phone Number	Comments

INDEPENDENT (SPECIAL) TRUSTEE:

When we create a trust intended to shelter the unified credit of the first to die (these are often called credit shelter, family, or disclaimer trusts) we usually want the trust to benefit the surviving spouse first and the children second. Keeping property ownership out of the hands of the survivor is the primary means in eliminating the tax. For people who are not spending nearly all of the income they are receiving now, it may be that the surviving spouse will never want the money or income from this trust. But if they want more than the income, they will need an independent trustee to serve with them as co-trustees of the deceased spouse's trust. As mentioned in the information about HEMS, we need the trustee to approve of certain withdrawals and their purposes to avoid having the income beneficiary become the owner of the trust's assets. This person should be someone you trust (obviously) as well as someone you can get along with and have easy access to. They will have a duty to the remainder beneficiaries (your children/grandchildren) and may occasionally not agree with you, but they will have to have a reason because you can and should give yourself the right to remove and replace them if they do not act in your best interest.

Independent (Special) Trustee	Phone Number	Comments

TRUSTEE:

The primary word here is *trust*. The Trustee stands in your shoes and makes the financial decisions you would make if you were here and confronted with the same facts and circumstances. Select someone who knows you well or whose judgment you trust completely. This person does not have to be a financial wizard but should have enough sense to hire someone when they need help. They will interact with the guardian and the children/grandchildren during the years there are trusts in force. This could be a long time. This person will make investments and give a reporting of the trusts assets as required. They will help make decisions (and will have the final say) in what resources are released to the children/grandchildren for their health, education, maintenance and support (HEMS). To the extent you can give the trustee relatively clear guidance in the document, you will enable them to accurately reflect your values and wishes and will cut down on conflict between them and the beneficiaries. This person could have the expanded role of educating your children/grandchildren in the areas of money and investing (Lord knows they would need it if the two of you were not here and left this sort of money to them). Many people write a substantial narrative that lays out their philosophies about money, philanthropy, the dangers of "easy wealth," investing, business and the like. This is normally separate from the will itself and serves as a guidepost for your children/grandchildren and your trustee. I strongly believe we ought to condense these values and beliefs to writing for the benefit of creating our financial planning "constitution" to serve as a guide to our trustees as well as our children and ourselves. It is also interesting to revisit our narrative from time to time in an effort to see what has changed, and why, then reflect those changes in an updated statement.

Trustee Names	Phone Number	Comments

STANDARD PROVISIONS:

Wills and/or Trusts will have some "Standard Provisions" that affect you a great deal; and many that will not. The focus here is on the primary issues.

The document will provide for the personal representative (PR) to pay all doctor and funeral bills, and typically all debts, as well. **DANGER-POTENTIAL TRAP**: This may not always be in the best interest of your trustee or your children/grandchildren. If you are investing in real estate, the trustee may want to maintain those properties and the leverage created by those investments. Remember that trusts created by your will for the benefit of others have a taxpayer identification number and pay their own tax; pretty aggressively, I might add. The tax benefits created by your debt-encumbered property will be very beneficial in managing your estate. Consider modifying this provision to give the personal representative discretion as to which debts to retire, and which to maintain. There is a potential trap here if you own property and want it paid off. First, the dollars used to pay the debt will reduce the amount available to provide for the children/grandchildren (at least on a near-term basis) and often your personal representative would create a tax in accessing the cash assets. IRA's and other "qualified" plans are subject to income tax in respect of the decedent and would be taxed immediately if liquidated to pay off the debt. This combination of factors could cause your trustee and PR to sell your real estate (all with new basis based on today's rules -- see estate maximization through real estate), which may be the least favorable alternative.

The provisions that follow will distribute the assets remaining in the estate. Remember, your estate can only hold that which was owned by the decedent after his/her death -- all joint property, IRAs and insurance policies to which the survivor is the beneficiary are not included in the estate of the decedent for "disposition" purposes.

Usually all personal property except any "special" personal property noted in a written list, is passed to the spouse. Many people attach a written list giving certain items to certain people (my son gets this gun, my daughter gets that antique doll, that sort of thing).

There will be an Article that says something to the effect, "I will give to my family trust (credit shelter) the amount allowed by law without creating an estate tax ($1,000,000). The income from this trust shall be paid to my spouse and he or she is free to access the principal of this trust principal for their health, education, maintenance and support (HEMS). After my spouse's death, the assets will be distributed according to 'Article four'."

The idea behind this trust is to make the maximum use of a married couple's unified credit. You can leave as much as you want to each other via the unlimited marital deduction, so we tend to fill up this "family trust" in whatever manner makes the most sense.

Health, Education, Maintenance and Support (HEMS):

The HEMS provisions serve at least two important purposes in our wills and trusts. First, they help create a basis of discussion between the trustee and the guardian. The guardian will provide explanations of expenses that the trusts ought to pay for, and together the trustee and guardian will develop a policy for dealing with the expenses of raising your children/ grandchildren. I always encourage young families to buy enough insurance to make sure there is plenty of money available to make this a smooth process. It can be obtained so cheaply for most people it seems like such a waste for there to be financial challenges in addition to the fact the children/grandchildren's parents are gone.

The second and potentially the most legally important purpose for HEMS are to create an ascertainable standard by which the beneficiary can access the principal of the trust. Let's say your spouse dies and there is money transferred into their trust in an effort to maximize the tax opportunities for your family. We know that if you own all the money outright there is the potential for higher estate taxes in your situation. You are to receive all the income from this trust and can access (through an independent trustee) the principal *for HEMS*. Virtually any expense can be considered HEMS if all parties agree (Independent trustee and beneficiary), but we cannot give the income beneficiary unlimited access to the principal, otherwise it would be deemed owned by the beneficiary and would lose its benefit from an estate tax perspective as well as its creditor-proof status.

Disclaimers:

Another tool that your attorney might employ to fund this trust is a disclaimer. A disclaimer works in this way: "I will leave all of my assets to my spouse except that which they may disclaim, which will constitute the disclaimer trust, and shall be governed by the provisions of Article Four."

Disclaimers are especially useful when the family relationship is right because it gives a person so much flexibility. But they seem particularly useful in a time of extremely volatile tax law. One gets to choose in the rear view mirror which assets to populate the family trust with, and how much, based on the law in effect at the time of the first death. The danger in this environment is that there may be some period of time when there is no tax at all and the survivor might decide not to put any money in the "family trust." This could be devastating if the tax is reinstated during the lifetime of the survivor.

There is another two-fold advantage of funding the family trust regardless of the legislative condition at the time of the first death. As the first to die, you can be reasonably assured that a substantial portion of your resources will be distributed via your wishes and that those assets will be largely creditor-proof until the trusts are terminated.

As the survivor, you get the increased flexibility and peace of mind in knowing that those resources are earmarked for your kids. You have freedom when it comes to entering into new relationships in the sense you can be more generous, or at least less worried about sharing resources with a new spouse. You can go beyond the family trust with this type of planning if you both feel strongly about this subject.

DISTRIBUTION TO CHILDREN:

There will be an Article (usually number Four) which spells out the provisions for distributions to your children/ grandchildren should your spouse not survive you. This is pretty big deal. Many people don't give this enough consideration and provide for HEMS until 25 and then distribute the assets outright to the children/grandchildren. For most 25-year-olds this is a bad idea. I have attached to the following graphics a series of ideas to help you build a distribution ladder that will impact your children and, potentially, grandchildren.

DISTRIBUTION LADDERS:

By the time our children/grandchildren are adults we have a pretty good feel for their abilities and limitations in managing and spending money. Many of the people I work with have what I would call "stable adult children." Often their initial thought is that they would leave the money to their kids in equal proportions as soon as it is convenient after their collective deaths. What if the child is in the middle of a divorce or is soon to be? Parents often don't truly know the marital status of their kids. What about a lawsuit or some other major issue? Wouldn't it be prudent to give them a chance to right the ship before we give them the money? I often ask a client, "If your child/grandchild won the lottery, even a small one, would you want them to run right down to the lotto office to collect, or would you want them to take the time to breathe and think about what they were doing?" When you give the children/grandchildren an outright distribution you take away their ability to do that. The following is a short ladder that allows the children/grandchildren a chance to take advantage of the wealth relatively quickly, while protecting them today from unforeseen circumstances in the future. Remember that if your child/grandchild has a "hot investment" or a business he or she is focused in, they can work with the trustee to incorporate that into the trust investment mix. They just cannot take the money and spend it on nothing. It will be invested, and they can have some say in how.

SAMPLE DISTRIBUTION FOR STABLE ADULT CHILDREN:

Distribute to our children/grandchildren then living, as soon as is practical after our death, one third of the distributable assets as defined in Article X. At the end of the third year after the date of our death, distribute one-half of the balance of the assets to our children/grandchildren divided equally. At the end of the fifth year, distribute the remainder. Any income produced during the terms of the trust should be paid proportionately to each child/grandchild at least annually.

You can, of course, change it to two and four years or eight or ten, it is completely up to you.

For people with young children/grandchildren the situation is more complicated. In the area on Guardians, we discussed how gifts to children/grandchildren can balloon to amounts much larger than anticipated. This is not in and of itself a bad thing, but one has to decide how to address it.

The next series of ladder options deals with gifts from a trust for education. Some people would choose to pay for all post-secondary educational expenses, some would choose to limit the gift and create conditions under which the trust can be accessed.

EDUCATIONAL PROVISIONS:

Each child/grandchild may be provided, at the discretion of the trustee, funds used to pay for tuition fees, room and board, paid directly to the institution. This may continue for up to five years.

☐ Each child/grandchild may be provided, at the discretion of the trustee, the amount of ten thousand dollars adjusted by the COI beginning in 2003 dollars to pay for tuition fees, room and board, paid directly to the institution. This may continue for up to five years.

☐ A child/grandchild will achieve at least a 2.5 GPA for funding to continue. The trustee shall have discretion to make exceptions under special circumstances.

☐ A child/grandchild may go to post graduate school with the trust's help if they achieve a 3.0 GPA in the last two years of college.

☐ If the child/grandchild goes to nursing, teaching, or religious school (pick your favorite) they will receive full support if they

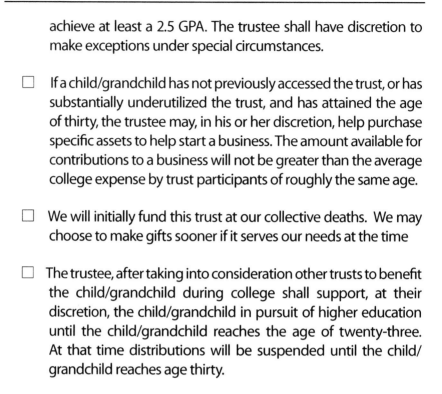

achieve at least a 2.5 GPA. The trustee shall have discretion to make exceptions under special circumstances.

☐ If a child/grandchild has not previously accessed the trust, or has substantially underutilized the trust, and has attained the age of thirty, the trustee may, in his or her discretion, help purchase specific assets to help start a business. The amount available for contributions to a business will not be greater than the average college expense by trust participants of roughly the same age.

☐ We will initially fund this trust at our collective deaths. We may choose to make gifts sooner if it serves our needs at the time

☐ The trustee, after taking into consideration other trusts to benefit the child/grandchild during college shall support, at their discretion, the child/grandchild in pursuit of higher education until the child/grandchild reaches the age of twenty-three. At that time distributions will be suspended until the child/grandchild reaches age thirty.

Trusts that eventually distribute their principal to your children or grandchildren need to be handled differently. People all too often end these trusts at age 23 or 25 or 30 without thinking through the amounts of money or the benefits of the assets remaining in trust. People often think of assets being held in trust as being controlled from beyond the grave. But what can a trustee not do that the beneficiary cannot do? If the child wants to have income property, can they not purchase it in the trust? Investments in stocks, or even investments in a business, can be made by the trust for the benefit of your child/grandchild. If the child wants to purchase a recreational property and the trustee thought it made sense based on the overall situation, the trust could certainly own it and the child benefit from it. With that in mind, look at some of these simple options.

TRUSTS THAT EVENTUALLY DISTRIBUTE THEIR PRINCIPAL:

☐   Upon reaching the age of thirty the trustee shall pay to the children/grandchildren, then living, twenty percent (20%) of the trust's assets, upon reaching age thirty-five the trustee shall distribute twenty-five percent (25%) of the trust's assets. Upon reaching age forty the trustee will distribute thirty-five percent (35%) of its assets. Upon reaching age forty-five, the trust will distribute fifty percent (50%) of its assets with the balance at age fifty. The trustee will always have discretion to pass income along to the beneficiary, but the intent of the trust is to create gifts at intervals, rather than creating an income stream.

☐   If any child/grandchild is the beneficiary of a trust due to the death of a parent, the trustee shall make distributions as follows:

☐   In coordination with the guardian for health, education, maintenance and support, until the youngest child of the deceased child reaches the age of eighteen. At that time the trusts will divide into separate trusts.

☐   The trustee, after taking into consideration other trusts to benefit the child/grandchild during college, shall support, at their discretion, the child/grandchild in pursuit of higher education until the child/grandchild reaches the age of twenty-three. At that time distributions will be suspended until the child/grandchild reaches age thirty, at which point the trustee shall distribute fifty percent of the trust's assets, with the balance to be distributed at the age of thirty-five.

UNIFIED CREDIT AND PROPERTY OWNERSHIP

From an estate tax perspective, nothing is more important than the unified credit and your ability to use it wisely.

Every American taxpayer has the "right:" To transfer $1,000,000 (not to be confused with annual gifts of $12,000 or less), living or dead to any one person, or any multiple of people they choose. If you are married you also have an unlimited marital deduction, which allows you to transfer as much as you want to your spouse. If you transfer all of your money to your spouse, when your spouse dies they have their $1,000,000 to give away. In that example, the unified credit of the "first to die" is wasted. If you set up a trust (as discussed in Chapter 10) the survivor can gain access to the assets of the trust and continue to benefit from the trust until his or her death. After the death of the surviving spouse the trust and its value will pass tax-free to the heirs along with the dead couple's assets, and the first $1,000,000 is tax free. This allows a married couple a total of $2,000,000 of tax-free transfers when done properly.

The estate tax law is in a massive state of flux at the moment. In 2006, as this is written, you can leave more than $1,000,000 tax-free once you have died, but only $1,000,000 while living. All of this reverts to $1,000,000, living or dead, in 2011. so I am assuming it is either after 2011 as you read this, or you will live at least that long. By then the numbers will likely have changed, so look into the new numbers if this concerns you. The action that you must take to make it possible for you to access this $2,000,000 or more of tax-free gifting comes in the form of reviewing the way you own your assets. Things that people tend to own jointly, like houses or cars, transfer directly to the surviving joint owner in almost all cases. This means that the deceased joint owner does not continue to own it after their death. If the transfer is to anyone other than the spouse, the deceased person's estate will recognize the gift that was made, as to the use of unified credit, but the deceased cannot give it to any person or trust other than the joint owner. Many other assets are subject to beneficiary designations like IRA's, insurance policies, annuity contracts and accounts labeled "payable on or transfer to upon death." These assets pass by contract, rather than through the Will, and as such are probate-free.

The bottom line is that you cannot give away that which you do not own. If you want an asset to be controlled by your Will you need to either own it or have the estate be the beneficiary of it. One caveat: You cannot transfer an IRA-type asset to anyone other than your spouse without his or her consent, and the tax consequences are such that you generally do not want them to be left to anyone else. We usually consider the IRA assets to be in the estate of the last to die, and work from there.

There are some fairly complex arrangements you can create regarding the beneficiaries and "stretching" of these assets, but most of the time you can consider them to be your most vulnerable assets from an estate tax perspective (they are taxable in the estate and income taxable to the heirs, often requiring the sale [or acquisition of] non IRA assets to pay the estate tax.) Most people would be well served to incorporate the IRA into the income plan and intend to exhaust it before life expectancy. If your IRA is too large to reasonably be spent, there are some excellent ways that you can use these assets to bolster the size of your estate and/or charitable giving (you could contact our firm if you desire more information). The planning around these techniques is so situational that it seems counterproductive to elaborate on the fundamentals here. It requires a certain expertise and I wouldn't want folks trying it on their own.

Creating proper property ownership, along with the use of unified credit, is the most powerful tax reduction tool we have of any type. The estate tax is the most aggressive tax anyone encounters, and its reduction is the most impactful of all.

Many of the ideas we have been discussing use modified forms of property ownership to create their results. Hopefully some of these will apply to you or someone you would seek to add value to.

So, what have we learned?

The **Uniform Prudent Investor Act** tells us to consider all factors relevant to the trust in order to make the most suitable investment decisions. This narrative has talked a great deal about creating leverage and positive inertia.

Offensive Tax Reduction is the art of taking the dollars you are already spending and making them tax deductible or creating assets that are tax effective and efficient.

Defensive Tax Reduction is the art of taking the assets you already own and making them tax efficient from an income, capital gains and estate tax perspective.

Creating effective financial plans involves taking what you already have, your relationships, skills, passions, fears and actual assets, and making them efficient from a wealth creation perspective.

We could go on in this forum discussing a great number of potentially complex tools and strategies that may or may not apply to your situation. I will avoid this for a few reasons. First, the more advanced tools require just the right blend of assets to facilitate. More art than science, as it were. More advanced tools also apply to fewer and fewer people based on the aforementioned asset requirements. The information becomes difficult to read and follow as there are many moving parts to consider. And lastly, you could make a mistake, which can be *extremely* expensive when dealing with complexity and larger dollar amounts. Our website www.creativewealthstrategies. com has more expanded information on various tools.

What hopefully has been clearly conveyed is that you have options. The foundation has long existed (in the form of the UPIA) for you to develop a lasting, significant financial constitution that will create the boundaries inside of which you can build your effective financial plan. You have all of the resources and relationships necessary to succeed. There are books and programs on the market that will give you the fundamental knowledge necessary to create success in any venture. There are financial tools and advisors that can cause you to manage your risk, increase your return, create more effective debt, and minimize the taxes due on the money you are already spending. You can and should create or position your wealth in such a way as to minimize tax on the monies you intend to spend, both now and in the future. You can acquire assets that will create both current and future benefits. There are ways you can protect your assets from creditors while reducing the effects of taxation in your estate, and there are processes you can put into place to increase the financial intelligence within your family for generations to come.

That is enough for one sitting. Now you must act. Do it now, do it now, and do it NOW.

Persist until you succeed my friends.

UNIFORM PRUDENT INVESTOR ACT

Drafted by the

NATIONAL CONFERENCE OF COMMISSIONERS ON UNIFORM STATE LAWS

and by it

APPROVED AND RECOMMENDED FOR ENACTMENT IN ALL THE STATES

at its

ANNUAL CONFERENCE MEETING IN ITS ONE-HUNDRED-AND-THIRD YEAR IN CHICAGO, ILLINOIS

JULY 29 - AUGUST 5, 1994

WITH PREFATORY NOTE AND COMMENTS

APPROVED BY THE AMERICAN BAR ASSOCIATION MIAMI, FLORIDA, FEBRUARY 14, 1995

UNIFORM PRUDENT INVESTOR ACT

The Committee that acted for the National Conference of Commissioners on Uniform State Laws in preparing the Uniform Prudent Investor Act was as follows:

RICHARD V. WELLMAN, University of Georgia, School of Law, Athens, GA 30602,
Chair

CLARKE A. GRAVEL, P.O. Box 369, 76 St. Paul Street, Burlington, VT 05402

JOHN H. LANGBEIN, Yale Law School, P.O. Box 208215, New Haven, CT 06520,
National Conference Reporter

ROBERT A. STEIN, American Bar Association, 750 North Lake Shore Drive, Chicago, IL 60611

EX OFFICIO

RICHARD C. HITE, 200 West Douglas Avenue, Suite 630, Wichita, KS 67202,
President

JOHN H. LANGBEIN, Yale Law School, P.O. Box 208215, New Haven, CT 06520,
CHAIR, DIVISION D

EXECUTIVE DIRECTOR

FRED H. MILLER, University of Oklahoma, College of Law, 300 Timberdell Road, Norman, OK 73019,
Executive Director

WILLIAM J. PIERCE, 1505 Roxbury Road, Ann Arbor, MI 48104,
Executive Director Emeritus

REVIEW COMMITTEE

EDWARD F. LOWRY, JR., Suite 1040, 6900 East Camelback Road, Scottsdale, AZ 85251, *Chair*

H. REESE HANSEN, Brigham Young University, J. Reuben Clark Law School, 348-A JRCB, Provo, UT 84602

MILDRED W. ROBINSON, University of Virginia, School of Law, 580 Massie Road, Charlottesville, VA 22903

ADVISOR TO DRAFTING COMMITTEE

JOSEPH KARTIGANER,
American Bar Association

Copies of this Act may be obtained from:

NATIONAL CONFERENCE OF COMMISSIONERS ON UNIFORM STATE LAWS

676 North St. Clair Street, Suite 1700

Chicago, Illinois 60611

312/915-0195

UNIFORM PRUDENT INVESTOR ACT

PREFATORY NOTE

Over the quarter century from the late 1960's the investment practices of fiduciaries experienced significant change. The Uniform Prudent Investor Act (UPIA) undertakes to update trust investment law in recognition of the alterations that have occurred in investment practice. These changes have occurred under the influence of a large and broadly accepted body of empirical and theoretical knowledge about the behavior of capital markets, often described as "modern portfolio theory."

This Act draws upon the revised standards for prudent trust investment promulgated by the American Law Institute in its Restatement (Third) of Trusts: Prudent Investor Rule (1992) [hereinafter Restatement of Trusts 3d: Prudent Investor Rule; also referred to as 1992 Restatement].

Objectives of the Act. UPIA makes five fundamental alterations in the former criteria for prudent investing. All are to be found in the Restatement of Trusts 3d: Prudent Investor Rule.

(1) The standard of prudence is applied to any investment as part of the total portfolio, rather than to individual investments. In the trust setting the term "portfolio" embraces all the trust's assets. UPIA § 2(b).

(2) The tradeoff in all investing between risk and return is identified as the fiduciary's central consideration. UPIA § 2(b).

(3) All categoric restrictions on types of investments have been abrogated; the trustee can invest in anything that plays an appropriate role in achieving the risk/return objectives of the trust and that meets the other requirements of prudent investing. UPIA § 2(e).

(4) The long familiar requirement that fiduciaries diversify their investments has been integrated into the definition of prudent investing. UPIA § 3.

(5) The much criticized former rule of trust law forbidding the trustee to delegate investment and management functions has been reversed. Delegation is now permitted, subject to safeguards. UPIA § 9.

Literature. These changes in trust investment law have been presaged in an extensive body of practical and scholarly writing. See especially the discussion and reporter's notes by Edward C. Halbach, Jr., in Restatement of Trusts 3d: Prudent Investor Rule (1992); see also Edward C. Halbach, Jr., Trust Investment Law in the Third Restatement, 27 Real Property, Probate & Trust J. 407 (1992); Bevis Longstreth, Modern Investment Management and the Prudent Man Rule (1986); Jeffrey N. Gordon, The Puzzling Persistence of the Constrained Prudent Man Rule, 62 N.Y.U.L. Rev. 52 (1987); John H. Langbein & Richard A. Posner, The Revolution in Trust Investment Law, 62 A.B.A.J. 887 (1976); Note, The Regulation of Risky Investments, 83 Harvard L. Rev. 603 (1970). A succinct account of the main findings of modern portfolio theory, written for lawyers, is Jonathan R. Macey, An Introduction to Modern Financial Theory (1991) (American College of Trust & Estate Counsel Foundation). A leading introductory text on modern portfolio theory is R.A. Brealey, An Introduction to Risk and Return from Common Stocks (2d ed. 1983).

Legislation. Most states have legislation governing trust-investment law. This Act promotes uniformity of state law on the basis of the new consensus reflected in the Restatement of Trusts 3d: Prudent Investor Rule. Some states have already acted. California, Delaware, Georgia, Minnesota, Tennessee, and Washington revised their prudent investor legislation to emphasize the total-portfolio standard of care in advance of the 1992 Restatement. These statutes are extracted and discussed in Restatement of Trusts 3d: Prudent Investor Rule § 227, reporter's note, at 60-66 (1992).

Drafters in Illinois in 1991 worked from the April 1990 "Proposed Final Draft" of the Restatement of Trusts 3d: Prudent Investor Rule and enacted legislation that is closely modeled on the new Restatement. 760 ILCS § 5/5 (prudent investing); and § 5/5.1 (delegation) (1992). As the Comments to this Uniform Prudent Investor Act reflect, the Act draws upon the Illinois statute in several sections. Virginia revised its prudent investor act in a similar vein in 1992. Virginia Code § 26-45.1 (prudent investing) (1992). Florida revised its statute in 1993. Florida Laws, ch. 93-257, amending Florida Statutes § 518.11 (prudent investing) and creating § 518.112 (delegation). New York legislation drawing on the new Restatement and on a preliminary version of this Uniform Prudent Investor Act was enacted in 1994. N.Y. Assembly Bill 11683-B, Ch. 609 (1994), adding Estates, Powers and Trusts Law § 11-2.3 (Prudent Investor Act).

Remedies. This Act does not undertake to address issues of remedy law or the computation of damages in trust matters. Remedies are the subject of a reasonably distinct body of doctrine. See generally Restatement (Second) of Trusts §§ 197-226A (1959) [hereinafter cited as Restatement of Trusts 2d; also referred to as 1959 Restatement].

Implications for charitable and pension trusts. This Act is centrally concerned with the investment responsibilities arising under the private gratuitous trust, which is the common vehicle for conditioned wealth transfer within the family. Nevertheless, the prudent investor rule also bears on charitable and pension trusts, among others. "In making investments of trust funds the trustee of a charitable trust is under a duty similar to that of the trustee of a private trust." Restatement of Trusts 2d § 389 (1959). The Employee Retirement Income Security Act (ERISA), the federal regulatory scheme for pension trusts enacted in 1974, absorbs trust-investment law through the prudence standard of ERISA § 404(a)(1)(B), 29 U.S.C. § 1104(a). The Supreme Court has said: "ERISA's legislative history confirms that the Act's fiduciary responsibility provisions 'codif[y] and mak[e] applicable to [ERISA] fiduciaries certain principles developed in the evolution of the law of trusts.'" *Firestone Tire & Rubber Co. v. Bruch*, 489 U.S. 101, 110-11 (1989) (footnote omitted).

Other fiduciary relationships. The Uniform Prudent Investor Act regulates the investment responsibilities of trustees. Other fiduciaries - such as executors, conservators, and guardians of the property - sometimes have responsibilities over assets that are governed by the standards of prudent investment. It will often be appropriate for states to adapt the law governing investment by trustees under this Act to these other fiduciary regimes, taking account of such changed circumstances as the relatively short duration of most executorships and the intensity of court supervision of conservators and guardians in some jurisdictions. The present Act does not undertake to adjust trust-investment law to the special circumstances of the state schemes for administering decedents' estates or conducting the affairs of protected persons.

Although the Uniform Prudent Investor Act by its terms applies to trusts and not to charitable corporations, the standards of the Act can be expected to inform the investment responsibilities of directors and officers of charitable corporations. As the 1992 Restatement observes, "the duties of the members of the governing board of a charitable corporation are generally similar to the duties of the trustee of a charitable trust." Restatement of Trusts 3d: Prudent Investor Rule § 379, Comment *b*, at 190 (1992). See also id. § 389, Comment *b*, at 190-91 (absent contrary statute or other provision, prudent investor rule applies to investment of funds held for charitable corporations).

SECTION 1.
PRUDENT INVESTOR RULE.

(a) Except as otherwise provided in subsection (b), a trustee who invests and manages trust assets owes a duty to the beneficiaries of the trust to comply with the prudent investor rule set forth in this [Act].

(b) The prudent investor rule, a default rule, may be expanded, restricted, eliminated, or otherwise altered by the provisions of a trust. A trustee is not liable to a beneficiary to the extent that the trustee acted in reasonable reliance on the provisions of the trust.

COMMENT

This section imposes the obligation of prudence in the conduct of investment functions and identifies further sections of the Act that specify the attributes of prudent conduct.

Origins. The prudence standard for trust investing traces back to *Harvard College v. Amory*, 26 Mass. (9 Pick.) 446 (1830). Trustees should "observe how men of prudence, discretion and intelligence manage their own affairs, not in regard to speculation, but in regard to the permanent disposition of their funds, considering the probable income, as well as the probable safety of the capital to be invested." Id. at 461.

Prior legislation. The Model Prudent Man Rule Statute (1942), sponsored by the American Bankers Association, undertook to codify the language of the *Amory* case. See Mayo A. Shattuck, The Development of the Prudent Man Rule for Fiduciary

Investment in the United States in the Twentieth Century, 12 Ohio State L.J. 491, at 501 (1951); for the text of the model act, which inspired many state statutes, see id. at 508-09. Another prominent codification of the *Amory* standard is Uniform Probate Code § 7-302 (1969), which provides that "the trustee shall observe the standards in dealing with the trust assets that would be observed by a prudent man dealing with the property of another . . . ."

Congress has imposed a comparable prudence standard for the administration of pension and employee benefit trusts in the Employee Retirement Income Security Act (ERISA), enacted in 1974. ERISA § 404(a)(1)(B), 29 U.S.C. § 1104(a), provides that "a fiduciary shall discharge his duties with respect to a plan solely in the interest of the participants and beneficiaries and . . . with the care, skill, prudence, and diligence under the circumstances then prevailing that a prudent man acting in a like capacity and familiar with such matters would use in the conduct of an enterprise of like character and with like aims . . . ."

Prior Restatement. The Restatement of Trusts 2d (1959) also tracked the language of the *Amory* case: "In making investments of trust funds the trustee is under a duty to the beneficiary . . . to make such investments and only such investments as a prudent man would make of his own property having in view the preservation of the estate and the amount and regularity of the income to be derived . . . ." Restatement of Trusts 2d § 227 (1959).

Objective standard. The concept of prudence in the judicial opinions and legislation is essentially relational or comparative. It resembles in this respect the "reasonable person" rule of tort law. A prudent trustee behaves as other trustees similarly situated would behave. The standard is, therefore, objective rather than subjective. Sections 2 through 9 of this Act identify the main factors that bear on prudent investment behavior.

Variation. Almost all of the rules of trust law are default rules, that is, rules that the settlor may alter or abrogate. Subsection (b) carries forward this traditional attribute of trust law. Traditional trust law also allows the beneficiaries of the trust to excuse its performance, when they are all capable and not misinformed. Restatement of Trusts 2d § 216 (1959).

SECTION 2. STANDARD OF CARE; PORTFOLIO STRATEGY; RISK AND RETURN OBJECTIVES.

(a) A trustee shall invest and manage trust assets as a prudent investor would, by considering the purposes, terms, distribution requirements, and other circumstances of the trust. In satisfying this standard, the trustee shall exercise reasonable care, skill, and caution.

(b) A trustee's investment and management decisions respecting individual assets must be evaluated not in isolation but in the context of the trust portfolio as a whole and as a part of an overall investment strategy having risk and return objectives reasonably suited to the trust.

(c) Among circumstances that a trustee shall consider in investing and managing trust assets are such of the following as are relevant to the trust or its beneficiaries:

(1) general economic conditions;

(2) the possible effect of inflation or deflation;

(3) the expected tax consequences of investment decisions or strategies;

(4) the role that each investment or course of action plays within the overall trust portfolio, which may include financial assets, interests in closely held enterprises, tangible and intangible personal property, and real property;

(5) the expected total return from income and the appreciation of capital;

(6) other resources of the beneficiaries;

(7) needs for liquidity, regularity of income, and preservation or appreciation of capital; and

(8) an asset's special relationship or special value, if any, to the purposes of the trust or to one or more of the beneficiaries.

(d) A trustee shall make a reasonable effort to verify facts relevant to the investment and management of trust assets.

(e) A trustee may invest in any kind of property or type of investment consistent with the standards of this [Act].

(f) A trustee who has special skills or expertise, or is named trustee in reliance upon the trustee's representation that the trustee has special skills or expertise, has a duty to use those special skills or expertise.

COMMENT

Section 2 is the heart of the Act. Subsections (a), (b), and (c) are patterned loosely on the language of the Restatement of Trusts 3d: Prudent Investor Rule § 227 (1992), and on the 1991 Illinois statute, 760 § ILCS 5/5a (1992). Subsection (f) is derived from Uniform Probate Code § 7-302 (1969).

Objective standard. Subsection (a) of this Act carries forward the relational and objective standard made familiar in the *Amory* case, in earlier prudent investor legislation, and in the Restatements. Early formulations of the prudent person rule were sometimes troubled by the effort to distinguish between the standard of a prudent person investing for another and investing on his or her own account. The language of subsection (a), by relating the trustee's duty to "the purposes, terms, distribution requirements, and other circumstances of the trust," should put such questions to rest. The standard is the standard of the prudent investor similarly situated.

Portfolio standard. Subsection (b) emphasizes the consolidated portfolio standard for evaluating investment decisions. An investment that might be imprudent standing alone can become prudent if undertaken in sensible relation to other trust assets, or to other nontrust assets. In the trust setting the term "portfolio" embraces the entire trust estate.

Risk and return. Subsection (b) also sounds the main theme of modern investment practice, sensitivity to the risk/return curve. See generally the works cited in the Prefatory Note to this Act, under "Literature." Returns correlate strongly with risk, but tolerance for risk varies greatly with the financial and other circumstances of the investor, or in the case of a trust, with the purposes of the trust and the relevant circumstances of the beneficiaries. A trust whose main purpose is to support an elderly widow of modest means will have a lower risk tolerance than a trust to accumulate for a young scion of great wealth.

Subsection (b) of this Act follows Restatement of Trusts 3d: Prudent Investor Rule § 227(a), which provides that the standard of prudent investing "requires the exercise of reasonable care, skill, and caution, and is to be applied to investments not in isolation but in the context of the trust portfolio and as a part of an overall investment strategy, which should incorporate risk and return objectives reasonably suitable to the trust."

Factors affecting investment. Subsection (c) points to certain of the factors that commonly bear on risk/return preferences in fiduciary investing. This listing is nonexclusive. Tax considerations, such as preserving the stepped up basis on death under Internal Revenue Code § 1014 for low-basis assets, have traditionally been exceptionally important in estate planning for affluent persons. Under the present recognition rules of the federal income tax, taxable investors, including trust beneficiaries, are in general best served by an investment strategy that minimizes the taxation incident to portfolio turnover. See generally Robert H. Jeffrey & Robert D. Arnott, Is Your Alpha Big Enough to Cover Its Taxes?, Journal of Portfolio Management 15 (Spring 1993).

Another familiar example of how tax considerations bear upon trust investing: In a regime of pass-through taxation, it may be prudent for the trust to buy lower yielding tax-exempt securities for high-bracket taxpayers, whereas it would ordinarily be imprudent for the trustees of a charitable trust, whose income is tax exempt, to accept the lowered yields associated with tax-exempt securities.

When tax considerations affect beneficiaries differently, the trustee's duty of impartiality requires attention to the competing interests of each of them.

Subsection (c)(8), allowing the trustee to take into account any preferences of the beneficiaries respecting heirlooms or other prized assets, derives from the Illinois act, 760 ILCS § 5/5(a)(4) (1992).

Duty to monitor. Subsections (a) through (d) apply both to investing and managing trust assets. "Managing" embraces monitoring, that is, the trustee's continuing responsibility for oversight of the suitability of investments already made as well as the trustee's decisions respecting new investments.

Duty to investigate. Subsection (d) carries forward the traditional responsibility of the fiduciary investor to examine information likely to bear importantly on the value or the security of an investment - for example, audit reports or records of title. E.g., *Estate of Collins*, 72 Cal. App. 3d 663, 139 Cal. Rptr. 644 (1977) (trustees lent on a junior mortgage on unimproved real estate, failed to have land appraised, and accepted an unaudited financial statement; held liable for losses).

Abrogating categoric restrictions. Subsection 2(e) clarifies that no particular kind of property or type of investment is inherently imprudent. Traditional trust law was encumbered with a variety of categoric exclusions, such as prohibitions on junior mortgages or new ventures. In some states legislation created so-called "legal lists" of approved trust investments. The universe of investment products changes incessantly. Investments that were at one time thought too risky, such as equities, or more recently, futures, are now used in fiduciary portfolios. By contrast, the investment that was at one time thought ideal for trusts, the long-term bond, has been discovered to import a level of risk and volatility - in this case, inflation risk - that had not been anticipated. Accordingly, section 2(e) of this Act follows Restatement of Trusts 3d: Prudent Investor Rule in abrogating categoric restrictions. The Restatement says: "Specific investments or techniques are not per se prudent or imprudent. The riskiness of a specific property, and thus the propriety of its inclusion in the trust estate, is not judged in the abstract but in terms of its anticipated effect on the particular trust's portfolio." Restatement of Trusts 3d: Prudent Investor Rule § 227, Comment f, at 24 (1992). The premise of subsection 2(e) is that trust beneficiaries are better protected by the Act's emphasis on close attention to risk/return objectives as prescribed in subsection 2(b) than in attempts to identify categories of investment that are per se prudent or imprudent.

The Act impliedly disavows the emphasis in older law on avoiding "speculative" or "risky" investments. Low levels of risk may be appropriate in some trust settings but inappropriate in others. It is the trustee's task to invest at a risk level that is suitable to the purposes of the trust.

The abolition of categoric restrictions against types of investment in no way alters the trustee's conventional duty of loyalty, which is reiterated for the purposes of this Act in Section 5. For example, were the trustee to invest in a second mortgage on a piece of real property owned by the trustee, the investment would be wrongful on account of the trustee's breach of the duty to abstain from self-dealing, even though the investment would no longer automatically offend the former categoric restriction against fiduciary investments in junior mortgages.

Professional fiduciaries. The distinction taken in subsection (f) between amateur and professional trustees is familiar law. The prudent investor standard applies to a range of fiduciaries, from the most sophisticated professional investment management firms and corporate fiduciaries, to family members of minimal experience. Because the standard of prudence is relational, it follows that the standard for professional trustees is the standard of prudent professionals; for amateurs, it is the standard of prudent amateurs. Restatement of Trusts 2d § 174 (1959) provides: "The trustee is under a duty to the beneficiary in administering the trust to exercise such care and skill as a man of ordinary prudence would exercise in dealing with his own property; and if the trustee has or procures his appointment as trustee by representing that he has greater skill than that of a man of ordinary prudence, he is under a duty to exercise such skill." Case law strongly supports the concept of the higher standard of care for the trustee representing itself to be expert or professional. See Annot., Standard of Care Required of Trustee Representing Itself to Have Expert Knowledge or Skill, 91 A.L.R. 3d 904 (1979) & 1992 Supp. at 48-49.

The Drafting Committee declined the suggestion that the Act should create an exception to the prudent investor rule (or to the diversification requirement of Section 3) in the case of smaller trusts. The Committee believes that subsections (b) and (c) of the Act emphasize factors that are sensitive to the traits of small trusts; and that subsection (f) adjusts helpfully for the distinction between professional and amateur trusteeship. Furthermore, it is always open to the settlor of a trust under Section 1(b) of the Act to reduce the trustee's standard of care if the settlor deems such a step appropriate. The official comments to the 1992 Restatement observe that pooled investments, such as mutual funds and bank common trust funds, are especially suitable for small trusts. Restatement of Trusts 3d: Prudent Investor Rule

§ 227, Comments *h*, *m*, at 28, 51; reporter's note to Comment *g*, id. at 83.

Matters of proof. Although virtually all express trusts are created by written instrument, oral trusts are known, and accordingly, this Act presupposes no formal requirement that trust terms be in writing. When there is a written trust instrument, modern authority strongly favors allowing evidence extrinsic to the instrument to be consulted for the purpose of ascertaining the settlor's intent. See Uniform Probate Code § 2-601 (1990), Comment; Restatement (Third) of Property: Donative Transfers (Preliminary Draft No. 2, ch. 11, Sept. 11, 1992).

SECTION 3. DIVERSIFICATION.

A trustee shall diversify the investments of the trust unless the trustee reasonably determines that, because of special circumstances, the purposes of the trust are better served without diversifying.

COMMENT

The language of this section derives from Restatement of Trusts 2d § 228 (1959). ERISA insists upon a comparable rule for pension trusts. ERISA § 404(a)(1)(C), 29 U.S.C. § 1104(a)(1)(C). Case law overwhelmingly supports the duty to diversify. See Annot., Duty of Trustee to Diversify Investments, and Liability for Failure to Do So, 24 A.L.R. 3d 730 (1969) & 1992 Supp. at 78-79.

The 1992 Restatement of Trusts takes the significant step of integrating the diversification requirement into the concept of prudent investing. Section 227(b) of the 1992 Restatement treats diversification as one of the fundamental elements of prudent investing, replacing the separate section 228 of the Restatement of Trusts 2d. The message of the 1992 Restatement, carried forward in Section 3 of this Act, is that prudent investing ordinarily requires diversification.

Circumstances can, however, overcome the duty to diversify. For example, if a tax-sensitive trust owns an underdiversified block of low-basis securities, the tax costs of recognizing the gain may outweigh the advantages of diversifying the holding. The wish to retain a family business is another situation in which the purposes of the trust sometimes override the conventional duty to diversify.

Rationale for diversification. "Diversification reduces risk . . . [because] stock price movements are not uniform. They are imperfectly correlated. This means that if one holds a well diversified portfolio, the gains in one investment will cancel out the losses in another." Jonathan R. Macey, An Introduction to Modern Financial Theory 20 (American College of Trust and Estate Counsel Foundation, 1991). For example, during the Arab oil embargo of 1973, international oil stocks suffered declines, but the shares of domestic oil producers and coal companies benefitted. Holding a broad enough portfolio allowed the investor to set off, to some extent, the losses associated with the embargo.

Modern portfolio theory divides risk into the categories of "compensated" and "uncompensated" risk. The risk of owning shares in a mature and well-managed company in a settled industry is less than the risk of owning shares in a start-up high-technology venture. The investor requires a higher expected return to induce the investor to bear the greater risk of disappointment associated with the start-up firm. This is compensated risk - the firm pays the investor for bearing the risk. By contrast, nobody pays the investor for owning too few stocks. The investor who owned only international oils in 1973 was running a risk that could have been reduced by having configured the portfolio differently - to include investments in different industries. This is uncompensated risk - nobody pays the investor for owning shares in too few industries and too few companies. Risk that can be eliminated by adding different stocks (or bonds) is uncompensated risk. The object of diversification is to minimize this uncompensated risk of having too few investments. "As long as stock prices do not move exactly together, the risk of a diversified portfolio will be less than the average risk of the separate holdings." R.A. Brealey, An Introduction to Risk and Return from Common Stocks 103 (2d ed. 1983).

There is no automatic rule for identifying how much diversification is enough. The 1992 Restatement says: "Significant diversification advantages can be achieved with a small number of well-selected securities representing different industries . . . . Broader diversification is usually to be preferred in trust investing," and pooled investment vehicles "make thorough diversification practical for most trustees." Restatement of Trusts 3d: Prudent Investor Rule § 227, General Note on Comments *e-h*, at 77 (1992). See also Macey, supra, at 23-24; Brealey, supra, at 111-13.

Diversifying by pooling. It is difficult for a small trust fund to diversify thoroughly by constructing its own portfolio of individually selected investments. Transaction costs such as the round-lot (100 share) trading economies make it relatively expensive for a small investor to assemble a broad enough portfolio to minimize uncompensated risk. For this reason, pooled investment vehicles have become the main mechanism for facilitating diversification for the investment needs of smaller trusts.

Most states have legislation authorizing common trust funds; see 3 Austin W. Scott & William F. Fratcher, The Law of Trusts § 227.9, at 463-65 n.26 (4th ed. 1988) (collecting citations to state statutes). As of 1992, 35 states and the District of Columbia had enacted the Uniform Common Trust Fund Act (UCTFA) (1938), overcoming the rule against commingling trust assets and expressly enabling banks and trust companies to establish common trust funds. 7 Uniform Laws Ann. 1992 Supp. at 130 (schedule of adopting states). The Prefatory Note to the UCTFA explains: "The purposes of such a common or joint investment fund are to diversify the investment of the several trusts and thus spread the risk of loss, and to make it easy to invest any amount of trust funds quickly and with a small amount of trouble." 7 Uniform Laws Ann. 402 (1985).

Fiduciary investing in mutual funds. Trusts can also achieve diversification by investing in mutual funds. See Restatement of Trusts 3d: Prudent Investor Rule, § 227, Comment *m*, at 99-100 (1992) (endorsing trust investment in mutual funds). ERISA § 401(b)(1), 29 U.S.C. § 1101(b)(1), expressly authorizes pension trusts to invest in mutual funds, identified as securities "issued by an investment company registered under the Investment Company Act of 1940 . . . ."

SECTION 4. DUTIES AT INCEPTION OF TRUSTEESHIP.

Within a reasonable time after accepting a trusteeship or receiving trust assets, a trustee shall review the trust assets and make and implement decisions concerning the retention and disposition of assets, in order to bring the trust portfolio into compliance with the purposes, terms, distribution requirements, and other circumstances of the trust, and with the requirements of this [Act].

COMMENT

Section 4, requiring the trustee to dispose of unsuitable assets within a reasonable time, is old law, codified in Restatement of Trusts 3d: Prudent Investor Rule § 229 (1992), lightly revising Restatement of Trusts 2d § 230 (1959). The duty extends as well to investments that were proper when purchased but subsequently become improper. Restatement of Trusts 2d § 231 (1959). The same standards apply to successor trustees, see Restatement of Trusts 2d § 196 (1959).

The question of what period of time is reasonable turns on the totality of factors affecting the asset and the trust. The 1959 Restatement took the view that "[o]rdinarily any time within a year is reasonable, but under some circumstances a year may be too long a time and under other circumstances a trustee is not liable although he fails to effect the conversion for more than a year." Restatement of Trusts 2d § 230, comment *b* (1959). The 1992 Restatement retreated from this rule of thumb, saying, "No positive rule can be stated with respect to what constitutes a reasonable time for the sale or exchange of securities." Restatement of Trusts 3d: Prudent Investor Rule § 229, comment *b* (1992).

The criteria and circumstances identified in Section 2 of this Act as bearing upon the prudence of decisions to invest and manage trust assets also pertain to the prudence of decisions to retain or dispose of inception assets under this section.

SECTION 5. LOYALTY.

A trustee shall invest and manage the trust assets solely in the interest of the beneficiaries.

COMMENT

The duty of loyalty is perhaps the most characteristic rule of trust law, requiring the trustee to act exclusively for the beneficiaries, as opposed to acting for the trustee's own interest or that of third parties. The language of Section 4 of this Act derives from Restatement of Trusts 3d: Prudent Investor Rule § 170 (1992), which makes minute changes in Restatement of Trusts 2d § 170 (1959).

The concept that the duty of prudence in trust administration, especially in investing and managing trust assets, entails adherence to the duty of loyalty is familiar. ERISA § 404(a)(1)(B), 29 U.S.C. § 1104(a)(1)(B), extracted in the Comment to Section

1 of this Act, effectively merges the requirements of prudence and loyalty. A fiduciary cannot be prudent in the conduct of investment functions if the fiduciary is sacrificing the interests of the beneficiaries.

The duty of loyalty is not limited to settings entailing self-dealing or conflict of interest in which the trustee would benefit personally from the trust. "The trustee is under a duty to the beneficiary in administering the trust not to be guided by the interest of any third person. Thus, it is improper for the trustee to sell trust property to a third person for the purpose of benefitting the third person rather than the trust." Restatement of Trusts 2d § 170, comment *q*, at 371 (1959).

No form of so-called "social investing" is consistent with the duty of loyalty if the investment activity entails sacrificing the interests of trust beneficiaries - for example, by accepting below-market returns - in favor of the interests of the persons supposedly benefitted by pursuing the particular social cause. See, e.g., John H. Langbein & Richard Posner, Social Investing and the Law of Trusts, 79 Michigan L. Rev. 72, 96-97 (1980) (collecting authority). For pension trust assets, see generally Ian D. Lanoff, The Social Investment of Private Pension Plan Assets: May it Be Done Lawfully under ERISA?, 31 Labor L.J. 387 (1980). Commentators supporting social investing tend to concede the overriding force of the duty of loyalty. They argue instead that particular schemes of social investing may not result in below-market returns. See, e.g., Marcia O'Brien Hylton, "Socially Responsible" Investing: Doing Good Versus Doing Well in an Inefficient Market, 42 American U.L. Rev. 1 (1992). In 1994 the Department of Labor issued an Interpretive Bulletin reviewing its prior analysis of social investing questions and reiterating that pension trust fiduciaries may invest only in conformity with the prudence and loyalty standards of ERISA §§ 403-404. Interpretive Bulletin 94-1, 59 Fed. Regis. 32606 (Jun. 22, 1994), to be codified as 29 CFR § 2509.94-1. The Bulletin reminds fiduciary investors that they are prohibited from "subordinat[ing] the interests of participants and beneficiaries in their retirement income to unrelated objectives."

SECTION 6. IMPARTIALITY.

If a trust has two or more beneficiaries, the trustee shall act impartially in investing and managing the trust assets, taking into account any differing interests of the beneficiaries.

COMMENT

The duty of impartiality derives from the duty of loyalty. When the trustee owes duties to more than one beneficiary, loyalty requires the trustee to respect the interests of all the beneficiaries. Prudence in investing and administration requires the trustee to take account of the interests of all the beneficiaries for whom the trustee is acting, especially the conflicts between the interests of beneficiaries interested in income and those interested in principal.

The language of Section 6 derives from Restatement of Trusts 2d § 183 (1959); see also id., § 232. Multiple beneficiaries may be beneficiaries in succession (such as life and remainder interests) or beneficiaries with simultaneous interests (as when the income interest in a trust is being divided among several beneficiaries).

The trustee's duty of impartiality commonly affects the conduct of investment and management functions in the sphere of principal and income allocations. This Act prescribes no regime for allocating receipts and expenses. The details of such allocations are commonly handled under specialized legislation, such as the Revised Uniform Principal and Income Act (1962) (which is presently under study by the Uniform Law Commission with a view toward further revision).

SECTION 7. INVESTMENT COSTS.

In investing and managing trust assets, a trustee may only incur costs that are appropriate and reasonable in relation to the assets, the purposes of the trust, and the skills of the trustee.

COMMENT

Wasting beneficiaries' money is imprudent. In devising and implementing strategies for the investment and management of trust assets, trustees are obliged to minimize costs.

The language of Section 7 derives from Restatement of Trusts 2d § 188 (1959). The Restatement of Trusts 3d says: "Concerns over compensation and other charges are not an obstacle to a reasonable course of action using mutual funds and other pooling arrangements, but they do require special attention by a trustee. . . . [I]t is important for trustees to make careful cost comparisons, particularly among similar products of a specific type being considered for a trust portfolio." Restatement of Trusts 3d: Prudent Investor Rule § 227, comment *m*, at 58 (1992).

SECTION 8. REVIEWING COMPLIANCE.

Compliance with the prudent investor rule is determined in light of the facts and circumstances existing at the time of a trustee's decision or action and not by hindsight.

COMMENT

This section derives from the 1991 Illinois act, 760 ILCS 5/5(a)(2) (1992), which draws upon Restatement of Trusts 3d: Prudent Investor Rule § 227, comment *b*, at 11 (1992). Trustees are not insurers. Not every investment or management decision will turn out in the light of hindsight to have been successful. Hindsight is not the relevant standard. In the language of law and economics, the standard is ex ante, not ex post.

SECTION 9. DELEGATION OF INVESTMENT AND MANAGEMENT FUNCTIONS.

(a) A trustee may delegate investment and management functions that a prudent trustee of comparable skills could properly delegate under the circumstances. The trustee shall exercise reasonable care, skill, and caution in:

(1) selecting an agent;

(2) establishing the scope and terms of the delegation, consistent with the purposes and terms of the trust; and

(3) periodically reviewing the agent's actions in order to monitor the agent's performance and compliance with the terms of the delegation.

(b) In performing a delegated function, an agent owes a duty to the trust to exercise reasonable care to comply with the terms of the delegation.

(c) A trustee who complies with the requirements of subsection (a) is not liable to the beneficiaries or to the trust for the decisions or actions of the agent to whom the function was delegated.

(d) By accepting the delegation of a trust function from the trustee of a trust that is subject to the law of this State, an agent submits to the jurisdiction of the courts of this State.

COMMENT

This section of the Act reverses the much-criticized rule that forbad trustees to delegate investment and management functions. The language of this section is derived from Restatement of Trusts 3d: Prudent Investor Rule § 171 (1992), discussed infra, and from the 1991 Illinois act, 760 ILCS § 5/5.1(b), (c) (1992).

Former law. The former nondelegation rule survived into the 1959 Restatement: "The trustee is under a duty to the beneficiary not to delegate to others the doing of acts which the trustee can reasonably be required personally to perform." The rule put a premium on the frequently arbitrary task of distinguishing discretionary functions that were thought to be nondelegable from supposedly ministerial functions that the trustee was allowed to delegate. Restatement of Trusts 2d § 171 (1959).

The Restatement of Trusts 2d admitted in a comment that "There is not a clear-cut line dividing the acts which a trustee can properly delegate from those which he cannot properly delegate." Instead, the comment directed attention to a list of factors that "may be of importance: (1) the amount of discretion involved; (2) the value and character of the property involved; (3) whether the property is principal or income; (4) the proximity or remoteness of the subject matter of the trust; (5) the character of the act as one involving professional skill or facilities possessed or not possessed by the trustee himself." Restatement of Trusts 2d § 171, comment *d* (1959). The 1959 Restatement further said: "A trustee cannot properly delegate to another power to select investments." Restatement of Trusts 2d § 171, comment *h* (1959).

For discussion and criticism of the former rule see William L. Cary & Craig B. Bright, The Delegation of Investment Responsibility for Endowment Funds, 74 Columbia L. Rev. 207 (1974); John H. Langbein & Richard A. Posner, Market Funds and Trust-Investment Law, 1976 American Bar Foundation Research J. 1, 18-24.

The modern trend to favor delegation. The trend of subsequent legislation, culminating in the Restatement of Trusts 3d: Prudent Investor Rule, has been strongly hostile to the nondelegation rule. See John H. Langbein, Reversing the Nondelegation Rule of Trust-Investment Law, 59 Missouri L. Rev. 105 (1994).

The delegation rule of the Uniform Trustee Powers Act. The Uniform Trustee Powers Act (1964) effectively abrogates the nondelegation rule. It authorizes trustees "to employ persons, including attorneys, auditors, investment advisors, or agents, even if they are associated with the trustee, to advise or assist the trustee in the performance of his administrative duties; to act without independent investigation upon their recommendations; and instead of acting personally, to employ one or more agents to perform any act of administration, whether or not discretionary . . . ." Uniform Trustee Powers Act § 3(24), 7B Uniform Laws Ann. 743 (1985). The Act has been enacted in 16 states, see "Record of Passage of Uniform and Model Acts as of September 30, 1993," 1993-94 Reference Book of Uniform Law Commissioners (unpaginated, following page 111) (1993).

UMIFA's delegation rule. The Uniform Management of Institutional Funds Act (1972) (UMIFA), authorizes the governing boards of eleemosynary institutions, who are trustee-like fiduciaries, to delegate investment matters either to a committee of the board or to outside investment advisors, investment counsel, managers, banks, or trust companies. UMIFA § 5, 7A Uniform Laws Ann. 705 (1985). UMIFA has been enacted in 38 states, see "Record of Passage of Uniform and Model Acts as of September 30, 1993," 1993-94 Reference Book of Uniform Law Commissioners (unpaginated, following page 111) (1993).

ERISA's delegation rule. The Employee Retirement Income Security Act of 1974, the federal statute that prescribes fiduciary standards for investing the assets of pension and employee benefit plans, allows a pension or employee benefit plan to provide that "authority to manage, acquire or dispose of assets of the plan is delegated to one or more investment managers . . . ." ERISA § 403(a)(2), 29 U.S.C. § 1103(a)(2). Commentators have explained the rationale for ERISA's encouragement of delegation:

ERISA . . . invites the dissolution of unitary trusteeship. . . . ERISA's fractionation of traditional trusteeship reflects the complexity of the modern pension trust. Because millions, even billions of dollars can be involved, great care is required in investing and safekeeping plan assets. Administering such plans-computing and honoring benefit entitlements across decades of employment and retirement-is also a complex business. . . . Since, however, neither the sponsor nor any other single entity has a comparative advantage in performing all these functions, the tendency has been for pension plans to use a variety of specialized providers. A consulting actuary, a plan administration firm, or an insurance company may oversee the design of a plan and arrange for processing benefit claims. Investment industry professionals manage the portfolio (the largest plans spread their pension investments among dozens of money management firms).

John H. Langbein & Bruce A. Wolk, Pension and Employee Benefit Law 496 (1990).

The delegation rule of the 1992 Restatement. The Restatement of Trusts 3d: Prudent Investor Rule (1992) repeals the nondelegation rule of Restatement of Trusts 2d § 171 (1959), extracted supra, and replaces it with substitute text that reads:

§ 171. Duty with Respect to Delegation. A trustee has a duty personally to perform the responsibilities of trusteeship except as a prudent person might delegate those responsibilities to others. In deciding whether, to whom, and in what manner to delegate fiduciary authority in the administration of a trust, and thereafter in supervising agents, the trustee is under a duty to the beneficiaries to exercise fiduciary discretion and to act as a prudent person would act in similar circumstances.

Restatement of Trusts 3d: Prudent Investor Rule § 171 (1992). The 1992 Restatement integrates this delegation standard into the prudent investor rule of section 227, providing that "the trustee must . . . act with prudence in deciding whether and how to delegate to others . . . ." Restatement of Trusts 3d: Prudent Investor Rule § 227(c) (1992).

Protecting the beneficiary against unreasonable delegation. There is an intrinsic tension in trust law between granting trustees broad powers that facilitate flexible and efficient trust administration, on the one hand, and protecting trust beneficiaries from the misuse of such powers on the other hand. A broad set of trustees' powers, such as those found in most lawyer-drafted instruments and exemplified in the Uniform Trustees' Powers Act, permits the trustee to act vigorously and expeditiously to maximize the interests of the beneficiaries in a variety of transactions and administrative settings. Trust law relies upon the duties of loyalty and prudent administration, and upon procedural safeguards such as periodic accounting and the availability of judicial oversight, to prevent the misuse of these powers. Delegation, which is a species of trustee power, raises the same tension. If the trustee delegates effectively, the beneficiaries obtain the advantage of the agent's specialized investment skills or whatever other attributes induced the trustee to delegate. But if the trustee delegates to a knave or an incompetent, the delegation can work harm upon the beneficiaries.

Section 9 of the Uniform Prudent Investor Act is designed to strike the appropriate balance between the advantages and the hazards of delegation. Section 9 authorizes delegation under the limitations of subsections (a) and (b). Section 9(a) imposes duties of care, skill, and caution on the trustee in selecting the agent, in establishing the terms of the delegation, and in reviewing the agent's compliance.

The trustee's duties of care, skill, and caution in framing the terms of the delegation should protect the beneficiary against overbroad delegation. For example, a trustee could not prudently agree to an investment management agreement containing an exculpation clause that leaves the trust without recourse against reckless mismanagement. Leaving one's beneficiaries remediless against willful wrongdoing is inconsistent with the duty to use care and caution in formulating the terms of the delegation. This sense that it is imprudent to expose beneficiaries to broad exculpation clauses underlies both federal and state legislation restricting exculpation clauses, e.g.,

ERISA §§ 404(a)(1)(D), 410(a), 29 U.S.C. §§ 1104(a)(1)(D), 1110(a); New York Est. Powers Trusts Law § 11-1.7 (McKinney 1967).

Although subsection (c) of the Act exonerates the trustee from personal responsibility for the agent's conduct when the delegation satisfies the standards of subsection 9(a), subsection 9(b) makes the agent responsible to the trust. The beneficiaries of the trust can, therefore, rely upon the trustee to enforce the terms of the delegation.

Costs. The duty to minimize costs that is articulated in Section 7 of this Act applies to delegation as well as to other aspects of fiduciary investing. In deciding whether to delegate, the trustee must balance the projected benefits against the likely costs. Similarly, in deciding how to delegate, the trustee must take costs into account. The trustee must be alert to protect the beneficiary from "double dipping." If, for example, the trustee's regular compensation schedule presupposes that the trustee will conduct the investment management function, it should ordinarily follow that the trustee will lower its fee when delegating the investment function to an outside manager.

SECTION 10. LANGUAGE INVOKING STANDARD OF [ACT].

The following terms or comparable language in the provisions of a trust, unless otherwise limited or modified, authorizes any investment or strategy permitted under this [Act]: "investments permissible by law for investment of trust funds," "legal investments," "authorized investments," "using the judgment and care under the circumstances then prevailing that persons of prudence, discretion, and intelligence exercise in the management of their own affairs, not in regard to speculation but in regard to the permanent disposition of their funds, considering the probable income as well as the probable safety of their capital," "prudent man rule," "prudent trustee rule," "prudent person rule," and "prudent investor rule."

COMMENT

This provision is taken from the Illinois act, 760 ILCS § 5/5(d) (1992), and is meant to facilitate incorporation of the Act by means of the formulaic language commonly used in trust instruments.

SECTION 11. APPLICATION TO EXISTING TRUSTS.

This [Act] applies to trusts existing on and created after its effective date. As applied to trusts existing on its effective date, this [Act] governs only decisions or actions occurring after that date.

SECTION 12. UNIFORMITY OF APPLICATION AND CONSTRUCTION.

This [Act] shall be applied and construed to effectuate its general purpose to make uniform the law with respect to the subject of this [Act] among the States enacting it.

SECTION 13. SHORT TITLE.

This [Act] may be cited as the "[Name of Enacting State] Uniform Prudent Investor Act."

SECTION 14. SEVERABILITY.

If any provision of this [Act] or its application to any person or circumstance is held invalid, the invalidity does not affect other provisions or applications of this [Act] which can be given effect without the invalid provision or application, and to this end the provisions of this [Act] are severable.

Motivational & Financial Framed Stuff from

CREATIVE WEALTH STRATEGIES INC
Featuring: Classic Truths

Victory…Someday

You're the one who used to boast
That you'd achieve the uttermost,
Some day

You merely wished a show,
To demonstrate how much you know
And prove the distance you can go…

Another year we've just past through.
What new ideas came to you?
How many big things did you do?

Time…left twelve fresh months in your care
How many of them did you share
With opportunity and dare
Again, where you so often missed?

We do not find you on the list of Makers Good
Explain the fact!
Ah no, 'twas not the chance you lacked!
As usual-you failed to act!
– Herbert Kauffman

I bargained with life for a penny
And life would pay no more
However I begged at evening
When I counted my scanty store
For life is a just employer
It pays you what you ask,
But once you have set the wages,
Why you must bear the task.
I work for a menial's hire,
Only to learned dismayed,
That any wage I'd of asked of life,
Life would have willingly paid
– ..Jesse Bell Rittenhouse

THE OLIVE THE KING OF ALL
TREES, TAKES ONE HUNDRED
YEARS TO BEAR FRUIT YET
AN ONION PLANT IS OLD IN
NINE WEEKS. I HAVE LIVED
AS AN ONION PLANT AND IT
DOES NOT SUIT ME
—— OG MANDINO

I HEAR NOT THOSE
WHO WEEP AND COMPLAIN
FOR THEIR DISEASE IS CON-
TAGIOUS LET THEM JOIN
THE SHEEP, THE SLAUGHTER-
HOUSE OF FAILURE IS NOT
MY DESTINY
— OG MANDINO

WWW.CREATIVEWEALTHSTRATEGIES.COM

Motivational & Financial T-shirts from

CREATIVE WEALTH STRATEGIES INC

Featuring: Phrases from the Masters

AND MANY MORE!!

WWW.CREATIVEWEALTHSTRATEGIES.COM

FINALLY, A BENEFITS PACKAGE THAT TEACHES TIME TESTED WEALTH CREATION TECHNIQUES TO IT'S PARTICIPANTS.

NOW IT IS AVAILABLE TO YOU AND YOUR COMPANY!

FINANCIAL INTELLIGENCE BENEFITS PACKAGE™

THIS PACKAGE WILL TEACH YOU:

- How to implement modern portfolio theory
- Build effective wills and trusts for your family
- How to create an effective financial plan:
  - How to excel utilizing the assets you already have
  - Creating effective income plans
  - Offensive and defensive tax reduction
  - Transforming income into wealth
  - Minimizing estate taxes

Did you know...

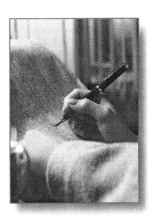

INVESTORS ARE MOTIVATED BY GREED AND FEAR—NOT BY SOUND INVESTMENT PRACTICES. *Dalbar Study*

A FUND THAT **PERFORMS AT 60%** OF THE S&P BEATS THE AVERAGE EQUITY INVESTOR. *Dalbar Study*

LESS THAN 1% OF ALL MONIES IN TAX DEFERRED INVESTMENTS ARE ACTIVELY MANAGED *Journal Financial Services Professionals*

70% OF AMERICANS DIE WITHOUT A WILL *Society of Will Writers*

67% OF AMERICAN BABY BOOMERS DO NOT HAVE ADEQUATE RETIREMENT SAVINGS *Population and Economic Review*

CREATE THE BENEFITS OF FINANCIAL INTELLIGENCE FOR YOURSELF!

Through the Financial Intelligence Benefits Package and the Uniform Prudent Investments Act (UPIA), you now have a proven effective alternative.

FINANCIAL INTELLIGENCE BENEFITS PACKAGE™

| CUSTOM INTRO DVD'S | Introduction to Modern Portfolio Theory |

ASSET MANAGEMENT
Experienced team implements Modern Portfolio Theory — Ongoing Communication

FINANCIAL FREEDOM DVD
DVD develops essentials for creating a successful financial plan

MPT DVD
DVD on how Modern Portfolio Theory applies to your portfolio

DEVELOPING FINANCIAL INTELLIGENCE BOOK
Creating framework on many levels on successful financial future

WILLS & TRUST DVD
Teaches you how to have a will and/or trust created for the benefit of your family

ESTATE MAX THROUGH RE
Demonstrates how to take real estate assets and make them real estate tax efficient

WILL KIT
Used along with the Will & Trust DVD — The kit creates a legal format

CUSTOM PRESENTATIONS
Custom presentations that suit your business model

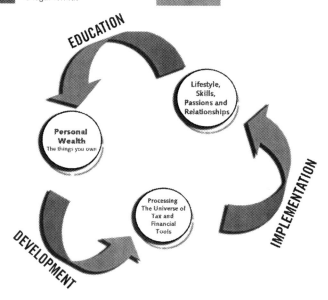

EDUCATION

Lifestyle, Skills, Passions and Relationships

Personal Wealth
The things you own

IMPLEMENTATION

Processing The Universe of Tax and Financial Tools

DEVELOPMENT

Creative Wealth Strategies
www.creativewealthstrategies.com

Printed in the United States
71654LV00004B/15